Stephen Leacock publishes *Sunshine Sketches of a Little Town.*

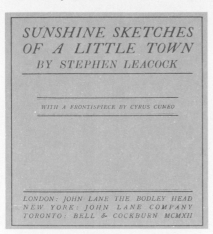

SUNSHINE SKETCHES
OF A LITTLE TOWN
BY STEPHEN LEACOCK

WITH A FRONTISPIECE BY CYRUS CUNEO

LONDON: JOHN LANE THE BODLEY HEAD
NEW YORK: JOHN LANE COMPANY
TORONTO: BELL & COCKBURN MCMXII

First Calgary Stampede.

Canada's first artificial ice arenas used for professional hockey in Vancouver and Victoria.

S.S. *Titanic* sinks after collision with iceberg off Newfoundland; 1,595 lost.

1913

Immigration reaches all-time high–over 400,000 arrive in Canada.

IMPORTANT

FARMERS
FARM LABOURERS
AND
FEMALE DOMESTIC
SERVANTS

ARE THE ONLY PEOPLE THE CANADIAN IMMIGRATION DEPARTMENT ADVISES TO EMIGRATE TO CANADA.

ALL OTHERS SHOULD GET DEFINITE ASSURANCE OF EMPLOYMENT IN CANADA BEFORE LEAVING HOME, AND HAVE MONEY ENOUGH TO SUPPORT THEM FOR A TIME IN CASE OF DISAPPOINTMENT.

Zippers become popular.

Fox trot becomes latest dance craze.

COMMENT SE DANSENT LES DANSES LES PLUS EN VOGUES !

Le "Fox-Trot" américain.

Arr...
incl...
Mil...

Stefa... Anderson begin five-year exploration of Arctic Canada.

Radio-Telegraph Act opens first stage of development of radio broadcasting in Canada.

1914

Great Britain declares war on Germany; Canada also at war.

LE DEVOIR

L'ANGLETERRE MOBILISERA DEMAIN

LA GUERRE   LA FRANCE VICTORIEUSE À LA FRONTIÈRE
COMBAT NAVAL DANS LA MER DU NORD

Canadian Expeditionary Force mobilizes at Valcartier, Que.

B.C. buys two submarines to defend the west coast.

S.S. *Komagata Maru* sails into Vancouver carrying 376 Indian Sikhs, who are refused entrance.

Turner Valley's Dingman Well in Alberta comes in.

Viking gas field in Alberta discovered.

S.S. *Empress of Ireland* sinks in Gulf of St. Lawrence; 1,024 lost.

IN MEMORIAM
OF
1024 SOULS LOST

EMPRESS OF IRELAND
MAY 29TH
1914

Montreal *Daily News* begins publication.

Henry Pellatt's mansion, Casa Loma, completed in Toronto.

Connaught Laboratories begin production of diphtheria antitoxin.

Louis Hémon publishes *Maria Chapdelaine.*

The Years of Agony

Above: *The "Princess Pats" became the best known Canadian unit in the British Army after their valiant but costly defence of the Belgian town of Ypres in 1915. War artist Richard Jack left nothing to the imagination in his blood-and-death depiction of their hand-to-hand combat with the enemy at the front.*

Previous page: *May 4, 1916, was K of K Day in Toronto. It was a day of patriotism, fund drives, recruiting rallies and a time to renew allegiance to the Empire. The southwestern Ontario town of Berlin was renamed Kitchener on this day to honour the illustrious British General, Sir Herbert Kitchener, Hero of Khartoum.*

John Craig
The Years of Agony
1910/1920

Canada's Illustrated Heritage

Canada's Illustrated Heritage

Publisher: Jack McClelland
Editorial Consultant: Pierre Berton
Historical Consultant: Michael Bliss
Editor-in-Chief: Toivo Kiil
Associate Editors: Clare McKeon
             Jean Stinson
Assistant Editors: Julie Dempsey
             Marta Howard
Design: William Hindle
       Lynn Campbell
       Neil Cochrane
Cover Artist: Alan Daniel
Picture Research: Lembi Buchanan
             Michel Doyon
             Judy Forman
             Betty Gibson
             Jonathan Hanna
             Margot Sainsbury

ISBN: 0-9196-4423-6

Copyright © 1977, Natural Science of Canada Limited.
All rights reserved. No part of this book may be
reproduced in any form or by any means, electronic,
mechanical, photocopying, recording, or otherwise,
without the prior written permission of the publisher.

N.S.L. Natural Science of Canada Limited
254 Bartley Drive
Toronto, Ontario M4A 1G4

Printed and bound in Canada

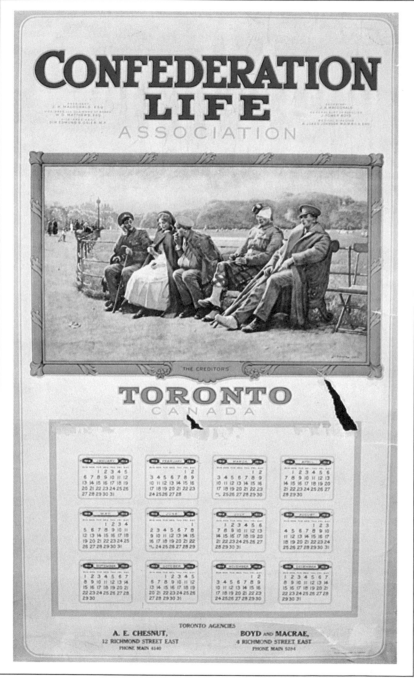

For many, the years of agony did not end with armistice on November 11, 1918.
Over 150,000 returned home wounded, some of them destined to spend the rest
of their days in veterans' hospitals, ever aware of the high cost of victory.

Contents

Days of Peace and Years of Agony

The world has drifted far from its old anchorage and no man can with certainty prophesy what the outcome will be.

Sir Robert Borden, 1914.

Near the border between France and Belgium, close by a town called Arras, there is a not very impressive height of land which overlooks the plains of Douai.

It is called Vimy Ridge.

At the crest, in a 248-acre park granted in perpetuity by the government of France, the twin towers of a magnificent monument rise starkly against the sky, visible for miles around in the peaceful, rural countryside. Massive in its dignity, ten years in the building, the monument was designed by Toronto sculptor Walter Allward, and unveiled by Edward VIII in the summer of 1936. The white stone used in its construction came from the shores of the Adriatic Sea, quarried from a site that had not been used since the time of the Roman Emperor Diocletian in the third century A.D.

At Vimy Ridge, in the chilly pre-dawn of April 9, the morning after Easter Sunday 1917, one hundred thousand Canadian soldiers launched an offensive against German positions that, for more than two years, had proved impregnable to all Allied assaults.

There, a half-dozen hours later, a brilliant victory had been achieved.

There, in that brief, terrible span of time, 3,524 Canadians died.

And there, it has often been said, Canada became a nation – a half-century after Confederation – at an obscure point on the map of western Europe, an ocean's width away from home.

The latter is, perhaps, too much to claim, for although Vimy Ridge will remain forever hallowed in the history of this country, it must share its page with a host of other obscure place names where Canadians also fought well and died with courage and distinction, in the Great War of 1914-1918. Ypres ... Courcelette ... Hill 70 ... the Somme ... the Marne ... Passchendaele ... Canal du Nord ... Cambrai. These little places, so far removed from other little places like Antigonish, Nova Scotia, and Valleyfield, Quebec, and Bowmanville, Ontario, and Carberry, Manitoba, and Saskatoon, Saskatchewan, and the Cariboo country of British Columbia, from whence the Canadian soldiers came.

They went into battle again and again, those Canadians, and they endured, and eventually they and the Allied armies that fought beside them– British, French, Anzac, American – won their war. Others of their kind, wearing the uniform of the British Royal Flying Corps, became air aces among the international elite of young men who created the tactics of aerial combat at a time when

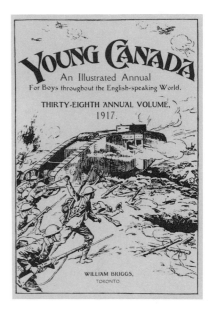

This 1917 Boys' Annual brought every feature of the war home for lads whose fathers and brothers were overseas.

Opposite page: *An exhausted soldier holds back sleep for a few minutes to write a letter home. His companions doze, cramped between trench walls.*

RANK	NAME	CASUALTIES
Sgt.	McDonald, M. F.	—
Gnr.	McDonald, W. M.	Wounded 1. 10. 16 Gassed 9. 8. 17 Wounded 2. 11. 17
Gnr.	McElary, V. D.	
Sig.	McEwan, J. N.	Gassed 18. 8. 17
Dr.	McIntyre, D. W.	
Bdr.	McIsaacs, J. A.	Wounded 2. 5. 15
Gnr.	McKay, A.	
Gnr.	McKay, A. J.	
Gnr.	McKenzie, A.	
A. Sgt.	McKenzie, S. A.	Wounded 1. 10. 16
A. Bdr.	McKinley, W. O.	
Gnr.	McKinnon, J. A.	Wounded 4. 5. 15 Gassed 18. 8. 17 Wounded 30. 3. 18
Dr.	McLean, F. J.	Killed in action 1. 8. 17
Dr.	McLean, H. E.	
Dr.	McLoughlin, H.	Wounded 21. 7. 16 Died 5. 8. 16
Gnt.	McMaster, D. J.	Wounded 2. 8. 17
A. Bdr.	McMurray, R. J.	Wounded 16. 8. 17
Gnr.	McMillan, F. J.	Wounded 19. 9. 16
Sgt.	McMillan, R. D.	Killed in action 10. 8. 18
Gnr.	McMullen, J.	Died of wounds 2. 5. 15
Gnr.	McMullen, L.	Gassed 18. 8. 17
Sig.	McNeil, O. B.	Wounded 21. 4. 17
Gnr.	McPhee, H	
Dr.	McQueen, F. F.	
Gnr.	McVey, J. P.	Wounded 23. 4. 15

A partial list of casualties of the 6th Battery, 2nd Brigade, Canadian Field Artillery. Formed in August, 1914, it fired its last round on Nov. 10, 1918.

the frontiers of flight itself had barely been crossed.

When the Armistice finally came, at 11 o'clock on November 11, 1918, restoring peace after what had become known as "the war to end all wars," no country had a better right to stand proud and rejoice in the victory than Canada. But the costs of that victory had been enormous.

Four long years of mud and blood, of filth and stench and rats and lice, of bloated corpses, of burrowing in the earth like animals, of shell shock and poison gas, of pain and deprivation and loneliness and rot and fear and carnage and horror.

Four long years of existing as men should never be asked or expected to live. Or die. At the end, 59,544 Canadians dead.

the legacy of war

The wounded came home, 172,950 of them, some blind, some with their minds destroyed, some lacking arms or legs, many doomed to spend the rest of their lives in veterans' hospitals from Halifax to Victoria.

What they came back to was a country that had changed in many important ways. If it is too romantic a notion to say that a nation was tempered and forged on the slopes of Vimy Ridge, there is no doubt that Canada became a very different homeland in the decade from 1910 to 1920.

The immediate legacy of the war, apart from the numbing casualties, included rampant inflation, widespread unemployment, and a coast-to-coast shortage of adequate, low-cost housing. Many a returning hero found himself without a job and without a decent place in which to live. But of far greater, long-range significance was the fact that the trial-by-ordeal of the Great War had revealed serious flaws and tears in the social and political fabric of the young nation. It had become clear that Confederation rested upon a complex of uneasy compromises: regional, class, cultural, linguistic, urban-rural, religious and, above all, emotional. Wherever the overseas veteran looked, he seemed to see only disharmony, tensions, struggles, demands and conflicting self-interests.

In 1910 the great majority of Canadians, secure and comfortable in a familiar and apparently ordered world, had looked forward to the future with confidence and optimism and, in many ways, with an almost child-like innocence.

the established order of things

At home, people understood and accepted their allotted roles in the scheme of things. Industrial and clerical workers expected to work long hours for low wages, and were grateful for the opportunity to put food into the bellies of their families, and to keep some kind of a roof over their heads. Farmers tilled their fields, and grew their crops, and took their produce to market, where they traditionally accepted going prices, however unfair, as having been established by some unidentified, greater authority which it was not in their province to question. Shopkeepers attended to their businesses with sharp eyes on their cash registers, and frequently with heavy thumbs on their scales. Women washed, ironed, swept, dusted, mended, mopped, baked, preserved, nursed, mothered and tended to the work that was never done. Politicians made election promises. The rich lived in big houses, got richer, filled the ranks of the professions with their sons, were decent employers and patient landlords, and contributed generously to churches and charities. It was God's will that it should be that way.

Abroad, the "mother country" could be counted upon to look after the best interests of the British Empire, including Canada, in the mysteri-

The Years of Agony

Above: The "Princess Pats" became the best known Canadian unit in the British Army after their valiant but costly defence of the Belgian town of Ypres in 1915. War artist Richard Jack left nothing to the imagination in his blood-and-death depiction of their hand-to-hand combat with the enemy at the front.

Previous page: May 4, 1916, was K of K Day in Toronto. It was a day of patriotism, fund drives, recruiting rallies and a time to renew allegiance to the Empire. The southwestern Ontario town of Berlin was renamed Kitchener on this day to honour the illustrious British General, Sir Herbert Kitchener, Hero of Khartoum.

ous world of foreign affairs. The King sat securely on his throne; Big Ben chimed every hour on the hour; the Foreign Office in Whitehall had the experience and the sophistication necessary to steer the ship of state through the shoals and reefs cast up by greedy, ambitious and distressingly perfidious foreign governments. And the mighty dreadnoughts of the Royal Navy cruised the seas and oceans of the world or lay at anchor in ports from Sydney, Australia, to Sydney, Nova Scotia.

In all of this the Canada of 1910 played little direct part. Ottawa was seldom consulted on matters of foreign policy, accepting with gratitude any information the Colonial Office might see fit to pass along. Canada was both legally and emotionally committed to stand behind whatever decisions were made in London. There might be some question as to the form such support should take, as in the mounting challenge created by the build-up of German naval power during the first decade of the twentieth century. But there was no doubt at all that it would be forthcoming. That, too, was part of the established order of things in 1910.

emergence from adolescence

A mere ten years later, having endured the horrors of war, and having contributed far more than its proportionate share towards final victory, Canada had earned the right to speak and be heard at international council tables. But with this emergence from adolescence came the disillusionments and harsh realizations which normally ac-

company adulthood.

By 1920 it was apparent that the nation which had responded so enthusiastically to the call of the "mother country" in 1914, and had seemed so united and unanimous in that response, was actually rent by internal dissensions that would continue far into the foreseeable future.

And it was equally clear that the empire's foreign policy could not safely be entrusted to the King's ministers in Whitehall and unquestioningly endorsed and supported by Ottawa; the price for that kind of blind acquiescence could be far, far too high.

Thus, by the end of the decade, Canadians were faced with the realization that they would have to work hard at learning to live together through typically uneasy and often grudging accommodations; and that, if it held together, their young nation must be responsible for its own survival in international diplomacy. England would remain a much loved and respected ancestor, but the relationship could no longer be one of mother and child; henceforth it would have to be an alliance between independent and equal partners.

By 1920 Canadians were forced to accept the fact that there was no externally imposed order; the world would be what nations and individuals could make of it, no more and no less.

There was no going back.

What had been, or what had seemed to be, belonged to the past, to yesterday . . . not to today, and certainly not to tomorrow. The years of innocence, like the years of agony, had become part of the national heritage.

The loss of life in the Great War was unprecedented and changed Canadian attitudes and values. Many of the fathers who did return home found that they could not begin their new lives with any enthusiasm or energy.

CHAPTER ONE

City Lights

The police commissioners are obliging all vehicles, abroad on Toronto streets after dark, to carry lights.

Saturday Night, 1911.

By 1910 the balance of population in Canada had begun to shift from rural to urban.

To be sure, the flood-tide of immigrants from Europe to Laurier's "last, best west" continued, and would not reach its peak until 1913, when just over 400,000 would pour into the country. More and more homesteads sprang up on the flat, endless prairies, and thousands of square miles of new land were brought under the plough and added to the wheat acreage.

But increasingly the new arrivals elected to stay in the older cities of eastern Canada or the burgeoning urban communities of the western provinces, rather than endure the lonely deprivation and back-breaking labour of "sod-busting." They were joined by growing numbers of their predecessors who, beaten by the brutal winters, late springs, early frosts and wind-blown emptiness, gave up and moved into the centres of population, where they would at least have near-by neighbours and a sense of community.

It was a trend that would continue so that, by the end of the decade, the population of the cities and towns would for the first time equal that of the rural areas.

By 1910 Montreal could claim a population of almost half a million (470,480). Toronto boasted 376,358 citizens. Halifax had 46,619. In the West, Calgary reached 55,000 and Regina, little more than an outpost in 1900, claimed 30,213. Vancouver, growing at the rate of 1,000 per month, neared 100,000.

Their citizens could point with pride to considerable civic progress. Electric streetcars, first introduced in the 1880s, had replaced horse-drawn trams in cities from Halifax to Victoria. In Toronto, Controller Horatio Hocken had even proposed the construction of a subway – a "harebrained" suggestion that was not to be taken seriously for some fifty years.

Mud-and-dust main streets were being paved, including Winnipeg's Portage Avenue, where the steam-rollers went to work in the spring of 1910. Many of them were lit by electricity at night, and Regina claimed to have the only illuminated street signs west of Toronto. In that same city the proprietor of a single-storey clothing emporium, impressed by the progress he saw on all sides, whimsically placed a sign in his window: "Elevator Boy Wanted!"

Automobiles were no longer a novelty. Durants, Locomobiles, Wintons, Columbias and Gasmobiles chugged along city streets, although the most popular make was the car already immortalized in the popular song "In My Merry

BUSINESS DOESN'T GROW. IT'S BUILT

Advertising firms like Rous & Mann solicited new business with slogans built on "boom-time" optimism.

Opposite page: Electric streetcars crowd Toronto's busy Yonge Street in 1915. A solitary motor car braves the traffic.

─GREAT AVIATION EXHIBITION─

EUGENE ELY

The world famous Anglo-American Aviator and
hero of several world-wide sensation creating flights
with his

CURTISS AEROPLANE

Aviation is the most modern and fascinating of the Sciences and the Aeroplane
the most ingenious and wonderful contrivance ever designed by man's mind or
fashioned by man's hand. Ely will give flights at

HENDERSON PARK, LETHBRIDGE

FRIDAY NEXT, JULY 14

Commencing at 1.30 p.m. and continuing throughout the afternoon. This is positively
the first exhibition in Western Canada of a flying machine operated by an experienced
and expert aviator. Ely will be seen in his famous

SPIRAL GLIDE AND OCEAN DIP

Two of the most daring and difficult feats ever performed by any airman

Weather conditions permitting, a

WELL KNOWN LOCAL YOUNG LADY

Will make a flight seated in Ely's biplane

ELY DAY IN LETHBRIDGE will be one of the Biggest Events ever
pulled off in Southern Alberta

ADMISSION 75 Cents Children under 12 years and accompanied
by their parents will be admitted free

Opening the splendid new $30,000 Main Exhibition Building

─WATCH FOR RAILROAD EXCURSION RATES─

*"Give me enough power and I'll fly
a barn door,"* barnstormer Eugene
Ely once quipped. He enthralled the
crowd at this Lethbridge, Alberta,
exhibition by taking a local lady
up–a daring feat in any weather.

Two intrepid flyers, Mr. & Mrs. Wm. McIntosh Stark of Vancouver, took to the air for a lesson in this Curtiss flying machine.

Oldsmobile." In Toronto you could buy a Model F two-cylinder Buick for $1,650. The number of auto agencies approximately equalled the number of livery stables in that city, where the police department had begun issuing parking tags back in 1907. In March of 1910 Dr. Whitelaw, Edmonton's Medical Health Officer, was fined $10 for speeding, having been clocked at 17 miles per hour!

In many cities, including Winnipeg, Ottawa and Victoria, "jitneys," private automobiles operating regular schedules at 5¢ a ride, were providing serious competition for the local streetcar systems.

No one thought that automobiles would ever be of much use during the winter months. Each late fall they were hoisted up on blocks in the family garage or barn, drained of their motor oil, and bedded down to await the coming of spring.

For the well-to-do and the comfortably-off

there was a flourishing and gratifying social life in the cities – private parties and military balls and social debuts and concerts and opening nights. Enrico Caruso appeared at the magnificent Massey Hall in Toronto. Sophie Tucker and Madame Schumann Heinck appeared in Regina. So did Barney Oldfield, the race-car driver, Buffalo Bill and Rube Marquard, the great baseball pitcher. Touring stage companies from New York and London travelled across the country and drew capacity houses wherever they appeared, especially in Vancouver, where the "theatre season" was a must for the socially ambitious.

High fashions were imported at premium prices from London, New York and Paris. Chiffon and satin were "in" that year of 1910. High, laced boots were still popular. The "vertical line" was the latest thing, with its narrow hobble skirts that were to shackle fashionable women for the next

12

Mechanical failures, poor roads, and a few inexperienced "nuts behind the wheel" created many spectacular road accidents.

"McKAY"

An Announcement of Our 1913 Model

40 h.p. car with Mohair top, windshield, electric lighting system dynamo and storage, Truffault-Hartford shock absorbers, electric horn, Stewart speedometer, and full set tools.

Seven passenger car with aluminum body   - $2300.00
Five Passenger   - $2050.00   Roadster   - $1950.00

30 h.p. car with Mohair top, windshield, speedometer, Truffault-Hartford shock absorbers, Presto tank, bulb horn, and full set tools.

Five passenger touring car   - $1585.00
Roadster   - $1485.00

A truly high grade car, and one that will compete in every detail with the highest priced cars on the market. Specially designed for rough roads.

THE TALK OF THE MONTREAL SHOW
Catalogue for the Asking

The Nova Scotia Carriage and Motor Car Co., Ltd.
Office and Factory————————————AMHERST, N.S.

Maritimers raised $2 million to build the McKay factory in Nova Scotia but in spite of promotional campaigns their automobile did not sell well. However, the all-aluminum body, mohair top and electric ignition and lighting made it "the talk of the Montreal show."

half-decade. Bustles were going out, and brassieres were gaining acceptance.

During the winters there was an endless round of dinners, dances, parties and grand balls for the social set. The waltz was still the basic step for debutantes and swains to master, but other dances were being introduced. Many of them – the fox-trot, the turkeytrot, the peacock strut – were named after birds and animals, presumably because they embodied a kind of mating routine. And the latest dance craze, the tango, imported from South America, was considered slightly naughty but was popular nonetheless.

Every month saw the completion of some imposing new building dedicated to culture, government, or higher learning. The Art Gallery opened in Toronto in the spring of 1910. The University of Saskatchewan was under construction in Saskatoon, where so recently buffalo had

swarmed. New legislative buildings were going up in Regina and Winnipeg, their size and elegance symptomatic of the expansive optimism of the time. Public libraries were springing up in cities from coast to coast. In Victoria the new Empress Hotel was attracting crowds of affluent tourists from near and far.

It was the last decade in which wealthy Canadians would build monuments to themselves. At Royal Roads, near Victoria, a magnificent castle, Hatley Park, which would soon become the residence of the Dunsmuir family, was under construction. And in Toronto Sir Henry Pellatt was considering plans for his Casa Loma. When it was finally completed in 1914, the baronial rooms and halls of this enormous structure, complete with secret passages, would be filled with rugs, tapestries, paintings and other treasures from all over the world. It would be the scene of lavish enter-

The escalator at Eaton's in Toronto was probably the first in Canada. Shoppers who ventured the "sliding staircase" in 1910 could celebrate the feat with a 5¢ ice cream cone.

tainments involving up to 3,000 guests.

Most homes had electric lights, and more and more upper-and middle-class families were enjoying the convenience of telephones. People were saying that you would soon be able to call long distance from Halifax to Victoria! Airplanes could no longer be dismissed as a "crackpot notion." True, an American, Charles F. Willard, had crashed into Lake Ontario three times the previous summer while trying to take off from Scarborough Beach, east of Toronto. But a month earlier J.A.D. McCurdy had made Canada's first successful flight at Baddeck, Nova Scotia. And in 1911 another American, Bob St. Henry, thrilled crowds at the Dominion Exhibition in Regina by taking off and landing in his 60-horsepower biplane– thereby inspiring many local youngsters who later became fine pilots.

Movies were taken for granted by then, but was it really possible, as some claimed, that there would one day be *talking* pictures? Or that this newfangled contraption called radio would let you listen to words and music from some distant city in your own home? It was hard to completely discount such far-fetched notions when things like gramophones, adding machines and vacuum-cleaners were already on the market.

cottages on wilderness islands

During this period Canadian urbanites, especially people of substance, many of whom had made their fortunes out of the primary resources of the country – grain on the Prairies, minerals and pulp and paper in Ontario and Quebec, timber in British Columbia, and railroads everywhere – were losing contact with the hinterlands beyond their cities, except in a few, very special ways. They welcomed the Saturday morning farmers' markets, characteristic of all provinces, which supplied them with fresh produce, eggs, fish, cord-wood and other staples at reasonable prices. And they built cottages on wilderness islands and shorelines – in the Muskoka and Kawartha Lakes in Ontario, in the Qu'Appelle Valley of Saskatchewan, in Quebec's Laurentians, along the Northwest Arm outside Halifax, on the mist-shrouded coasts near Vancouver and Victoria – to which they could escape during the oppressive heat of July and August.

a seamier side

Weekend commuting between city and summer cottage was a time-consuming proposition. Even affluent breadwinners and professional men put in a five-and-a-half-day week, so the exodus could not begin until Saturday noon. The outbound trip, which typically involved a journey by train followed by passage on a lake steamer, might well delay the weary traveller's re-union with his family until after dark. The return usually began in the pre-dawn hours of Monday morning. But it was just part of the orderly passing of the seasons for the city people who found most of their gratifications within the prosperous and increasingly more sophisticated urban communities they had been instrumental in creating.

There was, of course, a far less idyllic, much seamier side to all of this.

The rapid growth of Canada's urban centres had been a helter-skelter phenomenon, virtually without benefit of civic planning. The result was that, while every city had its fashionable district and boasted its monuments to culture, government and the good life, there were always slum districts, shanty-towns and depressed ghettos where life was nasty, brutish and short.

Predictably, services were slow in reaching these sections. In Winnipeg, for example, outhouses continued in use along North Main Street long after they had disappeared from Wellington Crescent. In Halifax, while streets in the genteel south end were flanked by flagstone or concrete sidewalks, ordinary citizens walked along paths of household cinders, spread by the city's collection wagons. In Toronto's Cabbagetown, residents still used communal wells, while upper-class Rosedale home-owners a few blocks away enjoyed filtrated tap water. In Regina's Germantown, 60 per cent of the houses were so poorly constructed that sewage and water connections could not be made. It was said that the most dangerous place in the western world in which to be born was the working-class section of Montreal, known as "the City below the Hill," where 26.8 per cent of all infants died within their first year.

blue serge suits for $5.95

The most serious shortage was a lack of adequate housing at rates that working men could afford. In the poorer districts of Halifax, Winnipeg, Calgary and Vancouver, some five-room houses contained as many as ten double beds. The *Regina Standard* reported that one night in March 1910, four hundred people had to walk the streets because they had nowhere to stay.

In most cities houses and flats rented to the working-class poor were owned by leading citizens from the residential districts, who not only gouged their tenants but also enjoyed the right to vote in every ward in which they owned property – an effective way of maintaining civic control.

Prices were low. In January 1910, men's blue serge suits were going for $5.95 in Toronto, where you could also buy a fine, oak rocking chair for $2.85, and sable muffs and stoles were being offered for $11. As for staple foods, Edmonton stores were featuring coffee at 40 cents a pound, round steak at 10 cents a pound, stewing beef at 6 cents, and canned apples at 35 cents a gallon.

Even so, wages had fallen behind. In Regina the average labourer earned just under $18 a week,

Competition during the First World War sent coal prices soaring. One company developed a coal-based fuel which it advertised in this jingle as being cheaper and easier to use than coal: "It hasn't got clinkers, it hasn't got slate, saves pain in the back by shaking the grate."

Help Wanted

Men and women working in offices and factories rose early in the morning and laboured into the evening, usually till six o'clock. Many endured the drudgery and boredom of piece-work, risking abuse from the shop foreman if they paused to talk. Labour unions were considered subversive, and no employee valuing his job would dare to talk openly about organizing for better wages and conditions. For most Canadians it was work six days a week (till noon on Saturday) and church on Sunday. Employers judged the deportment and moral character of job applicants–and their penmanship–before choosing the right person.

Wanted: Switchboard operator, one with typewriter experience preferred. Eaton's office in Toronto shows two women: a "typewriter" and a "hello girl."

Wanted: An experienced man to run small planing mill machine. Steady work. Mechanized equipment had replaced broadaxe-men of earlier decades.

Wanted: By western daily newspaper, a first-class circulation manager.
The Edmonton Daily Capital *editorial offices in 1912–a paper circus.*

Wanted: Superintendent for auto body factory. Must be first-class man.
By the end of the decade the first buses began to appear on main streets.

Wanted: Experienced operators to run power knitting and sewing machines.
Note the floor boss (centre) and the work clothes of these garment workers.

Wanted: Women to mail catalogues for mail order house–$15 weekly.
No men at the mail order desk of the Robert Simpson Company in 1910.

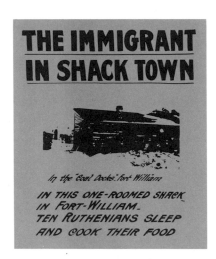

THE IMMIGRANT IN SHACK TOWN

In the 'Coal Docks', Fort William

IN THIS ONE-ROOMED SHACK IN FORT-WILLIAM TEN RUTHENIANS SLEEP AND COOK THEIR FOOD

Immigrants were lured to Canada in a campaign which had started at the end of the 19th century. But many of the newcomers, unaccustomed to the raw prairie winters and uncertain seasons, left their farms and sought work in the cities. On meagre wages few could get better shelter than the shanties on "the other side of the tracks."

and many were laid off for extended periods during the winter months. Montreal workers were even worse off – there the weekly average dropped almost to $10. Twenty cents an hour was the going wage in Halifax. Women were paid about half as much as men. Child labour was still common, although the minimum hiring age had recently been raised from twelve to fourteen years in most provinces. School teachers in rural Manitoba were paid $600 a year, out of which they were expected to pay for their room and board and sometimes required to buy coal or cord-wood to feed the pot-bellied stoves in their classrooms. For much of the year factory workers in Toronto and other industrial centres saw the sun only on Sundays. Most were at their machines from seven in the morning to five in the afternoon, six days a week, with a half-hour for lunch and no mid-morning or mid-afternoon breaks.

Trade unionism was making only slow and grudging progress. The Trades and Labour Congress and the competing Canadian Federation of Labour were encountering both the lethargy and timidity of workers and stiff resistance from employers, the Canadian Manufacturers' Association, most newspaper editors and the pulpit. "Working men have no right to organize to force their masters to pay higher wages" a prairie minister told his congregation, reflecting what may have been still a majority view of clergymen.

"all the beer you can drink"

Booze, sports and church – these were the opiates of the labouring poor. There were more saloons than there were downtown street corners in most cities and towns. There, long after the banks were closed, a working man could dip into his hard-earned pay envelope and take home whatever was left some hours later. Liquor and beer were cheap. In Regina the Kaiser Hotel in east-end

Germantown offered "all the beer you can drink" with the price of admission to its regular dances. West Indies' rum was "a quarter a quart" in Halifax, Fredericton and throughout the Maritimes. Along North Main Street in Winnipeg, where the swinging doors seldom closed and the sawdust covering the floors was replaced every morning, beer was a nickel, and whiskey ten cents or three for a quarter. Gin was not much more expensive than good drinking water in Toronto, and almost as plentiful. The forces of temperance were rallying, and within a few years would push through Prohibition in every province except Quebec; but in the meantime alcohol continued to be an escape for many depressed workers, and a curse for many hungry and impoverished wives and children.

push-cart coal-vendors

The bitter cold of Canadian winters imposed a particular burden on the working classes, the unemployed, the sick and the elderly. From October to May each year there was the constant, nagging need to find something to burn to keep warm – or at least warm enough to ward off colds, the 'flu, grippe, croup, catarrh and similar respiratory ailments from which many died each winter. In Halifax poor householders bought coal by the bushel from push-cart vendors ("Co! Cao! Co! Cao!"). In Toronto and other Ontario cities they haggled over the price of a half-cord of stove wood or slabs at the Saturday morning farmers' markets. In Winnipeg they shouted insults at firemen in passing locomotives, then harvested the chunks of anthracite and bunker-coal that were hurled at them. Keeping the heat up – splitting kindling, stoking and banking fires, taking out the ashes– was a constant problem, and vital to survival.

Of course colds came anyway. Hot goose grease rubbed on the neck, back and chest was

The Years of Agony

Above: *The "Princess Pats" became the best known Canadian unit in the British Army after their valiant but costly defence of the Belgian town of Ypres in 1915. War artist Richard Jack left nothing to the imagination in his blood-and-death depiction of their hand-to-hand combat with the enemy at the front.*

Previous page: *May 4, 1916, was K of K Day in Toronto. It was a day of patriotism, fund drives, recruiting rallies and a time to renew allegiance to the Empire. The southwestern Ontario town of Berlin was renamed Kitchener on this day to honour the illustrious British General, Sir Herbert Kitchener, Hero of Khartoum.*

Home Sweet Home? Living conditions in the north end of Winnipeg, 1915. A clothes line runs from door jamb to window, over the heads of nine cramped inhabitants.

A $2.00 BOOK FOR **ONLY $1.**⁰⁰

SEXUAL KNOWLEDGE

320 Pages ILLUSTRATED

By Dr. WINFIELD SCOTT HALL, Ph.D.

Noted Authority and Lecturer

PLAIN TRUTHS OF SEX LIFE—
What every young man and young woman, every young wife and young husband, every father and mother, teacher and nurse should know.

Sex Facts Hitherto Misunderstood

New Book All Need to Read
In plain wrapper for only $1.00; postage 10 cents extra.

On Sale at all Bookstores or from McClelland, Goodchild & Stewart Limited, Pub., 266 King St. W., Toronto.

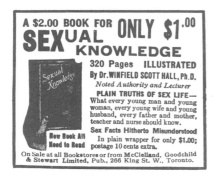

The reader is promised a greater understanding of sex by publishers McClelland, Goodchild and Stewart. Such books were not unusual even as early as the 1890s, but buyers expecting more than clinical drawings and moral sermonizing were in for a disappointment when they opened the plain brown mailing wrapper.

considered to be the most effective remedy, but it was usually available only after festive occasions like Thanksgiving and Christmas. At all other times the favourite was the old reliable mustard plaster. Powdered mustard was mixed with hot water, smeared on pieces of flannelette from old sheets or discarded underwear, and applied to the chest of the patient. For the first half-hour the potion would burn like a tablet delivered from Hell; after that, it would lay as dank, sodden and chill as the sod over a grave. Both sensations were well calculated to encourage the patient, cured or not, to vacate the sick bed at the earliest possible moment.

The well-to-do suffered from the rigours of winter too, but they had servants to bring them hot beef-tea and solicitous physicians to visit their bedsides.

By 1910 Canadian cities were maturing, and growing in sophistication as they grew in population. But the facade of progress, impressive though it was, masked much that was ugly and sordid, drew attention away from the squalor that often lay behind it, and provided a false front for a great many social injustices. While the mood of the country was buoyantly optimistic, it was clear that not all of the citizens of the still young Dominion would be allowed to share equally in its future.

This provided a fertile soil for the seeds of discontent which were being sown, and which would burst into vibrant bloom before the decade drew to a close.

Stiff and stern school mistresses keep an appraising eye on rows of young ladies learning the feminine arts. Better not miss a stitch!

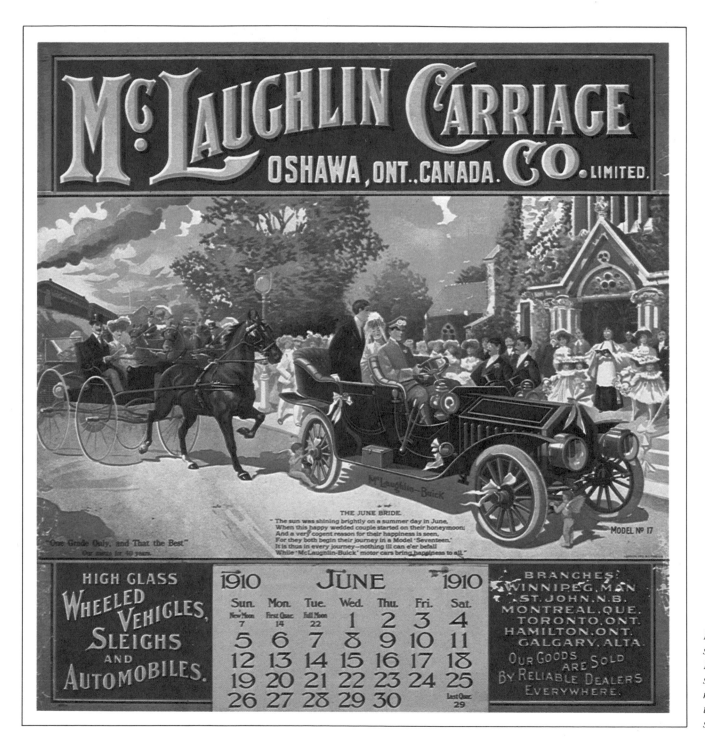

In calendar art of the period, nothing surpassed the stunning graphics of the McLaughlin Carriage Company, which showed off Colonel Sam's latest luxury model. Now they are a rare record of the fashions, manners and advertising style of the decade.

Fashion Plates

While most Canadians were shopping at Woodward's, The Bay, Eaton's or Simpson's for their clothes, fashion-minded ladies and gentlemen kept in step with changing styles by consulting the dressmakers' or haberdashers' "fashion plates." These large, hand-tinted engravings (opposite page) were issued quarterly and illustrated the vogue from Paris for women and from London for men.

The "peg top" style dominated women's fashion in the pre-war period. Brocade and silk "dusters" took their lines from ankle-length frocks.

SEASON'S GREETINGS
THE
KUNTZ BREWERY
LIMITED
WATERLOO, ONT. **

Taking the fashion cue from the American "Gibson Girl" look, the model in this Easter card shows the wide-brimmed plumed hat, the rage in bonnets.

Men's fashion underwent a dramatic change in 1910 with the introduction of the natural shoulder look. The slim trousers of the 19th century took on fullness in the leg but remained narrow at the ankle, a style most exaggerated in the "peg top" trouser of the first half of the decade. The overcoats shown above reflect the traditional British style in the full-cut Ulster (right and centre-right) and the tailored Chesterfield (left and centre-left). The derby was quite acceptable for business dress and the cap was a necessary appointment in motoring costumes. Low buttoned or laced shoes were fashionable for gentlemen, and shirt collars were detachable and rounded, stiff with starch or celluloid.

By 1910 the phonograph had become a fixture in the parlours of many Canadian homes. Double-sided disc recordings were rapidly replacing the cylinder, and the outside horn was slowly becoming a thing of the past. An evening's entertainment might consist of a rousing war song by the Imperial Quartet; a song of romance by Quebec lyric tenor Paul Dufault; choral music by the Mendelssohn Choir; Vesti La Giubba by the great young operatic tenor, Edward Johnson; the Empire Day address by the King and Queen; or a military band rendition of Louis-Phillippe Laurendeau's patriotic march, "Land of the Maple." Crank up the gramophone and listen.

CHAPTER TWO

A Weekend's Fun and Games

The effort to introduce such crude and vulgar forms of dancing as the "Tango" is becoming every day more widespread in Canada....

Saturday Night, 1913.

The pleasures most Canadians sought in 1910 were, by and large, simple ones. In spite of the growth of the cities and the impressive scientific and technological advances that had been made, the pace of life was still gentle – with promenades, strumming banjos, canoes and rowboats, tobogganing and the jingle of sleigh bells on crisp winter nights.

More than a half-century later, Mazo de la Roche, the famed creator of "Jalna," would remember the games boys and girls played then– London Bridge Is Falling Down, Here We Go Gathering Nuts in May, The Farmer Views His Lands, Hide-and-Seek and Old Witch.

It was a time for walking. To be sure, most Canadian cities had good, cheap street-railway systems by then, and a fair number of the well-to-do had automobiles, but the bicycle craze of the turn of the century had curiously faded and most citizens continued to use their feet and legs a great deal of the time. Fathers took their broods for walks on Sundays, before or after church; young men courted the objects of their affection during leisurely strolls; kids hiked to lakes and streams to camp and hunt and fish; housewives toddled off to corner stores and general stores and Saturday morning markets, with crocheted shopping bags in hand. And walking as a sport – the awkward-looking, heel-and-toe variety – drew huge crowds; Toronto's George Goulding was among the best in the world, and a young man named Walter Jackson, the Canadian boys' champion, was gaining recognition.

It was a time of steam – steam-rollers chugging and puffing over the hot asphalt on city streets; steam harvesters whistling and shaking in fields of golden grain; steam saws ripping out boards in lumber mills; and the giant, red, steam pumpers of the fire departments.

Steamboats were in their heyday – up and down the rivers and lakes, from Cape Breton's Ingonish to the inlets of Vancouver Island. Sunday school and lodge picnics. Moonlight excursions, with waltzes and fox-trots drifting over the silvered waters. The majestic, eighty-foot *Qu'Appelle,* with heated rooms, a handsome saloon, and splendid dining room, out of Regina. The *Turbinia, Dundurn, Cayuga* and *Kingston* taking crowds of happy excursionists from Toronto to Niagara Falls, Welland, Buffalo, Brockville, the Thousand Islands. Steamboat service from Halifax to McNab's Island. Steamers on Lake Winnipeg and Lake Manitoba. Paddle-wheelers along the endless miles of the Yukon. Steamers on the Kawarthas, the Muskokas, the Rideaus, the Lake of Two

Programme		
Extra		
1. Waltz		Forget-me-not
2. Medley One Step		Oui Oui Marie
3. Fox Trot		Everything
4. One Step		When You Come Back
5. Waltz		Kisses
6. One Step		Me-ow
7. Fox Trot		Smiles
8. Waltz		Roses of Picardy
9. Fox Trot		Darktown Strutters
10. One Step		Oh Frenchy
Supper Extras	1.	
	2.	
	3.	
11. One Step		Your'e In Style
12. Fox Trot		Jealous Moon
13. Waltz		My Paradise
14. Medley One Step		Howdy
15. Fox Trot		Tickle Toe
16. One Step		Katy
17. Waltz		Blue Rose
18. Fox Trot		Mother, Dixie And You
19. One Step		There's A Ship Bound For Blighty
20. Waltz		Perfect Day

The fox trot was the most popular dance step of the decade. However, this 1919 Victoria dance program makes no mention of the peacock strut, the bunny hug, the turkey trot or any of the other "barnyard" steps that were fads of the era.

Mary Pickford
Our Lady of the Silver Screen

Blue-eyed, golden-haired, innocent Gladys Smith was born in Toronto, April 8, 1893, and debuted onstage in *The Silver King* at age five. When her mother insisted she leave Broadway in 1909, she changed her name to Mary Pickford and went to Hollywood, where D.W. Griffith gave her a role in the silent film *The Violin Maker of Cremona* (1910). In her twenty years on the screen, she portrayed the innocent teenager. She won her first Academy Award for her first "talkie," *Coquette* (1929), and became "America's Sweetheart." When Griffith, Charlie Chaplin and Douglas Fairbanks (whom she later married) formed United Artists Corp., she was the financial and creative partner in the company behind its early success. Although she retired from the screen in 1935, she received a special award from the motion picture industry 40 years later for her outstanding work.

Mountains, the Saguenay, the Fraser.

Men and women in lonely farmhouses set their clocks by the whistles of steamboats. A boy whose family summered on Toronto's Centre Island was told to come home each evening when he heard the *Cayuga* whistle for the Eastern Gap. A dog at Young's Point, Ontario would sleep in the shade, oblivious of the ships passing by, until he heard the whistle of the *Islinda,* of which his master was the captain, when he would run, tail wagging, down to the locks.

And trains! The pencil lines of long freights inching slowly across the flat prairies. Great double-header locomotives labouring up through the passes of the Rockies. A conductor, fretting beside his train, taking his gold watch from the pocket of his blue serge vest. A few passengers, clustered around the pot-bellied stove in the waiting room of a small station on a cold morning, listening to the ticking of the clock and straining to hear the whistle of the milktrain far down the track. A small boy waiting until the first faint vibration signals that the Montreal to New York Express would soon be thundering by.

bandstands in the park

It was also a time for music. People listened to their new gramophones, which played cylindrical records and amplified the sound through large, conical horns. Harry Lauder was very popular. So was a song called "I Picked a Lemon in the Garden of Love, Where I Thought Only Peaches Grew." Other tunes being hummed and whistled included "I'm Always Chasing Rainbows," "After You've Gone," "I Wonder Who's Kissing Her Now," and "When You Were Sweet Sixteen."

Regina had held its first annual Saskatchewan Musical Festival the previous year, and the idea of encouraging young musicians by holding competitions with expert adjudicators quickly spread to Calgary, Vancouver, Winnipeg and other cities.

Sunday evening band concerts were popular in summer. Most towns and cities had bandstands in their parks, usually round or octagonal with ornate railings and "gingerbread" under the eaves, from which the local regimental band would play waltzes, marches, overtures and occasional selections from the classics. Old people sat on the park benches and listened; boys and girls darted through the shadows and pushed one another away from the water fountain; young men and women strolled and flirted under the whispering leaves and around the formal flower gardens.

the pit pianist and the silent films

Movies were still silent – but not without music. In the pit of the Grand Opera House in Peterborough, Ontario, Agnes Fenwick, a lady who had been a concert pianist and a member of the Royal Academy in her native England, glanced back and forth from the flickering screen above her to the cue sheet on her music stand, and accompanied the film with appropriate melodies. Her fingers would race as the hero chased the villain across the western plains, pound as the scene reached its climax, then become light and gentle on the keys when the mood changed from violent action to tender romance. When the performance was over she would assemble her music, switch off the light over her keyboard and go home to nurse her bedridden and partially paralyzed husband who, a few short years before, had been an important official in the pleasant city of Tunbridge Wells in "the old country." Every moviehouse had its piano player. However anonymous to the audiences, the pit pianist had to be good in order to learn a complete new score each week.

Outside of the movies and musical entertainments, there were stage companies from New

York and London, amateur theatre groups, vaudeville troupes and minstrel shows. Each year the Chautauqua, a touring extravaganza which originated in a town of that name in New York state, would pay its annual visit. The Chautauqua was a tent show and featured lectures by famous men–from Arctic explorers to literary figures to "Buffalo Bill" Cody – and melodramas designed to entertain the whole family. For many Canadians, the Chautauqua represented their first, and perhaps only, experience with the live stage. And one morning every summer small boys would get out of bed in the half-light before dawn to watch the circus train being shunted onto the railway siding. And perhaps, if they were lucky, to earn tickets to the matinee performance by carrying water to the elephants.

It was a time, too, when people liked to listen to speeches. Preachers were evaluated primarily on their ability to light the fires of Hell each Sunday morning; politicians were expected to provide at least part of the entertainment on public holidays; and horses were hitched to buggies for miles around whenever a famed orator such as the American William Jennings Bryan was scheduled to deliver an address.

time for reading

And it was a time when there was time for reading. Almost every city and town had a Carnegie public library. Stephen Leacock published *Literary Lapses* in 1910, followed by *Sunshine Sketches of a Little Town* two years later. The poems of Robert Service were much admired. Lucy Maud Montgomery's *Anne of Green Gables* was a Canadian bestseller. Bliss Carman, Charles G.D. Roberts and Ralph Connor were widely read. In Quebec William Henry Drummond amused English readers with "The Wreck of the Julie Plante," while the poets of the Ecole littéraire de

Silent films were the weekend feature in profusely ornamented theatres like the Comique in Toronto. Touring theatre companies found it too expensive to compete with the 5¢ admission price.

Sophisticated young men and women took to tennis despite the formal, hot and cumbersome sports clothing worn. These 1912 racketeers are from the Edson, Alberta, tennis club.

Curling was immensely popular. High in the Alberta Rockies it was played outdoors, where an ice patch could easily be cleared by sportsmen on a winter weekend.

Montréal – Desaulniers, Lozeau, Lemay, Garneau and others – were acclaimed by literate French Canadians.

It was a time, too, when moral standards were strict, and people across the country showed much concern for questions of propriety. In Toronto Kathleen Blake Watkins, who had earlier won fame as the world's first woman war correspondent in the Spanish-American conflict, devoted much of her weekly page in the *Mail and Empire* to answering letters from young women. Kit, as she liked to be called, seldom minced words, but never deigned to print the inquiries that prompted them. "I'd like to shake some sense into young married women like you, you are so stupid" she told a correspondent who had signed herself "Miserable." A consistent campaigner against padded bosoms, Kit replied to another letter-writer:

It is wrong of you, very wrong . . . Every girl should respect her own body absolutely. She should never permit herself to be kissed and embraced, even by a man old enough to be her great-grandfather. Faugh!

certain insanity

Each year thousands of Ontario school-boys were subjected to lectures by the Woman's Christian Temperance Union's official "Purity Agent," one Arthur W. Beall, a former missionary in Japan who had been recalled following a nervous breakdown. The main theme of Beall's "teaching" was the danger involved in bleeding away the life fluid from the male part, thus depriving the life glands of the vital secretions required to feed the brain and nervous system. Prolonged drainage, he warned, would lead to certain insanity and probable death.

Another influential source of "enlightenment" was the *Sex and Self* series, published in Philadel-phia and widely distributed in Canada by the Methodist church. This author, too, denounced "the solitary vice," from which grim consequences would surely ensue.

It might be supposed that such advice encouraged young men to keep their minds on other activities, such as games and contests.

a maximum of enthusiasm

In any event, it *was* a time for sports. People from all parts of the country and from all walks of life played them, watched them, talked about them, read about them in the newspapers. The well-to-do leaned towards the more genteel pursuits such as tennis, golf, badminton, croquet, cricket and polo. But in factories and bars, on street corners, verandahs and park benches, in barber shops, around general store heaters, wherever the mass of ordinary fans gathered, interest was chiefly in sports with more action and violence, like hockey, lacrosse, football, baseball and boxing.

Sports had, of course, played a part in the life of the young nation from its earliest days and before, back to the Indian game of *baggataway,* the forerunner of lacrosse. For a long time the games that took place were local or, at most, district affairs, played between amateur teams with a maximum of enthusiasm and a minimum of equipment. Hockey grew up on frozen canals, lakes, rivers and sloughs; baseball and football, like lacrosse, were played in open fields.

By 1910, however, the nature of sports was changing in Canada. They were becoming more organized and more commercial. Rule books were written. Leagues were formed, complete with constitutions and formal schedules. Trophies were donated. There were regional, provincial and even Dominion championships. Newspapers began to give much greater coverage to the contests, and

Kathleen Blake Watkins "Kit"

Internationally she was known as the first woman war correspondent and a top-notch reporter; but in Toronto she was known as "Kit"–Queen of the "sob sisters"–the woman who wrote the weekly advice to the lovelorn column. Kathleen Blake was born in Ireland in 1864, married at sixteen, and arrived in Canada, already a widow. When her second marriage broke up, she tried her hand at writing and landed a job with the *Toronto Mail and Empire*. For twenty years Kit wrote the weekly "Woman's Kingdom" page, eight columns of tiny type, answering personal, marital and sexual questions. As a globetrotting reporter she covered some of the major news stories of her time, from the 1893 Chicago World's Fair to the Spanish-American War. She fought her personal causes in the pages of the *Mail*–among them a campaign against women's corsets. She was the first president of the Canadian Women's Press Club, a post she held until her death in 1915.

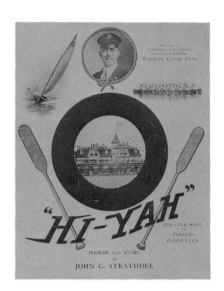

The "good years" created a boom in recreation, and Canadians by the thousand took an interest in all sorts of outdoor activities. In the cities, sports clubs sprang up and the locker rooms of the Toronto Canoe Club resounded with "Hi-Yah!"

Hurrah for this Winnipeg girls' baseball team called The White Hopes, among the first to invade the world of "men's sports."

some appointed sports editors to be responsible for this aspect of the passing parade. National sports heroes emerged. Arenas and enclosed baseball stadiums were built, and admissions were charged. Professionalism had begun to move in and was making rapid strides. Crowds increased as the number of spectators grew much more rapidly than the number of participants. Gambling became an increasingly common accompaniment– most of it taking place not through bookies, but as direct wagering between supporters of competing teams.

There were several reasons for these changes. As the population of the cities grew, there was a corresponding flowering in civic pride. One manifestation of this was a conviction that local teams could beat district rivals at hockey, baseball, lacrosse or football. Working men's hours were still long, but there was a gradual, grudging increase in leisure time, much of which was

devoted to watching sports. Wages were still low, but most labourers could come up with the price of a standing room ticket at least occasionally – and perhaps manage to get down a half-dollar bet on their favourite team as well.

The most important reason, however, was the progress that had been made in transportation. Not long before, games could only be arranged with neighbouring teams within the return range of horse-drawn stages, sleighs or wagons. By 1910, with the near-completion of the railway network, players could travel a hundred, even two hundred miles to play a game, and still get home in time, albeit sleepily, to report for work the following morning. A phenomenon of the period was the special train that took hundreds of cursing, carousing, hard-drinking fans to cheer for their favourites in play-off games against bitter rivals. It was the CPR, which had done so much to pull the country together, that made possible the national hockey

Every man and boy at the CNE grandstand is thinking "If I were in the driver's seat, they'd be watching me in the show!"

TOMMY BURNS

Will be home in a few days. He writes us that in all his travels he has never run across such smart clothes as

"Fashion Craft"

and he adds that for novelties and well selected furnishings

"Nothing has us beat."

Wait till he sees THE NEW 1912 SPRING RANGE that has kept us on the jump for the past two weeks

OPENING AND ARRANGING FOR YOUR INSPECTION.

The Suits, the Overcoats, the Hats, the Shirts, the Ties, etc.

THEY ARE HUMMERS

and Calgary's Best Dressed Men were never so pleased before.

Don't Miss Seeing The Last Word in Clothes.

Burns & Sewell

Calgary's Best Store for Fashion Craft Clothing and Correct Gents' Furnishings

130 Eighth Avenue West

Tommy Burns, Canada's only world heavyweight champion, retired after a brief return to boxing in 1910. Before turning evangelist he owned a Calgary clothing store, and his name alone gave sales a boost.

championship series each spring between teams from as far apart as Montreal or Toronto and Winnipeg, Regina, Calgary, Vancouver or, on one occasion, the far-distant Yukon.

Many sports vied for the attention of the fans. Most Canadians joined in following the exploits of the legendary Indian distance-runner, Tom Longboat – especially the series of brilliant races he ran against the Englishman, Alfie Shrubb. Longboat, a lanky Onondaga born on the Six Nations' Iroquois Reservation near Brantford, Ontario, drew huge crowds wherever he competed – like the multitude that packed Toronto's Centre Island to see him set a new world's record for 15 miles one summer afternoon in 1912.

Canada had some great boxers in the early part of the second decade of the twentieth century. Johnny Coulon, a native Torontonian, was the world's bantamweight champion from 1910 to 1914. Tommy Burns, the twelfth of thirteen chil-

dren born in a crude farmhouse near Hanover, Ontario, had announced his intention of returning to the ring after losing his heavyweight crown to Jack Johnson two years earlier. Another Canadian, Sam Langford, who ran away from his Weymouth, Nova Scotia home to become known professionally as the "Boston Tar Baby," was denied a much-deserved opportunity to win the heavyweight title because of his colour. Langford, a magnificent fighter who would die many years later, blind, destitute and forgotten, was not a victim of anti-black prejudices just in his adopted United States; in 1913, the boxing committee of the Amateur Athletic Union of Canada proclaimed that "no coloured boxer will be allowed to compete in the Canadian championships."

Lacrosse was a major sport across much of Canada. In Ontario, almost every city and town had at least one team. In Quebec, where it had first been brought to prominence by the Caugh-

**Sammy Langford
The Boston Tar Baby**

The boxing world was looking for the "Great White Hope" – someone to win back the heavyweight crown from Jack Johnson. A good many experts thought Sam Langford, a young boxer from Weymouth, N.S. – 5'4" with an 84" reach – was the only boxer who could flatten the champ. Langford was born in 1880, went to Boston in his teens, and started boxing in 1902. Because no division contender would meet him, he had to be satisfied fighting other blacks. He never got a crack at the crown. By 1923, Sammy Langford, totally blind in one eye, an alcoholic, could fight no longer. He quit boxing and died a nobody.

nawaga Indians, the game was summer's answer to hockey. It was popular in Manitoba and in the Maritimes, and to British Columbians it was the greatest game in the world. A professional league, with two teams in each of Montreal and Toronto, and franchises in Cornwall and Ottawa, seemed to be flourishing. But, beset by complaints of excessive violence, and challenged by other summer sports like baseball, cricket and soccer, its sun had passed its zenith and would all but set during the Great War of 1914-1918.

in the major leagues

The popularity of baseball, on the other hand, was growing. A number of Canadians were playing in the major leagues – Russell Ford of Brandon, Manitoba, with the New York Yankees; George "Moon" Gibson of London, Ontario, with the Pittsburgh Pirates; Larry McLean of Fredericton, New Brunswick, with the Cincinnati Redlegs. Gibson was an excellent catcher who helped Pittsburgh to defeat Detroit and the famed Ty Cobb in the World Series of 1909. Toronto had had a franchise in the prestigious International League since 1882, and many smaller cities like Peterborough and Kingston, Ontario, boasted professional or semi-professional teams – including Regina's marvellously named "Bonepilers" of the Class 'C' Western League.

Many good American players were glad to sign on with Canadian teams in exchange for room and board, part-time jobs that were not too onerous, and perhaps a few dollars left in their lockers from time to time. As the outlines of the diamond began to emerge from the snow each spring, fans would exchange rumours about what players the local club was going to import for the upcoming season. "I hear they're bringing in a right-hander from some place in Iowa . . . throws a fast-ball you can't even see, is what they say."

Football, a curious hybrid of soccer, English rugby, and American innovations, was gradually taking shape as an organized sport. The Interprovincial Rugby Football Union (eventually to become known as the "Big Four") had come into being in 1907, and two years later Albert Henry George, the fourth Earl Grey, had donated a cup to symbolize the national gridiron championship.

Canoeing, rowing, swimming, basketball (a game invented by a Canadian, James Naismith, in Springfield, Massachusetts in 1892), figure-skating, skiing, tennis – all of these sports had their enthusiastic advocates. Curling, the North American roots of which went back to eighteenth-century matches between Scottish merchants on the frozen St. Lawrence at Montreal, was growing in popularity, especially in the prairie provinces.

Golf, another import from Scotland, was also making giant strides, and by 1910 over fifty clubs had affiliated with the Royal Canadian Golf Association. The facilities, equipment and time required to play it, however, made it not a game for the ordinary working man.

the Queen's Plate

Horse racing had been part of the Canadian sporting scene since before Confederation, with the Queen's Plate, the oldest continuously run stakes in North America, dating from 1859. The thoroughbreds ran every summer at such tracks as Montreal's Blue Bonnets, Toronto's Carleton Club and Victoria's Beacon Hill. Standardbreds, the product of breeding fleet thoroughbreds with stronger work horses, raced on dusty, rutted ovals at summer fairs, and on the ice in winter from Charlottetown, Prince Edward Island, to the Red River at Winnipeg.

In the early years of the twentieth century horse racing was blatantly, often almost comically, corrupt. Bookies manipulated the odds; owners and

The judges in the stand are on their feet to watch the last lap of this motorcycle race in South Edmonton. Imagine a person travelling at the incredible speed of 60 miles per hour!

Ruffians of the Rink and Ring

Saturday afternoons sports fields and rinks across the country echoed with the boos and cheers of enthusiastic fans. Whether the action was a baseball game or a rugby-football match, the crowd was on its feet egging on the home team. It was an era of tough guys (and girls) and Canadian champs.

"Ruffians" of the rink at Rossland, B.C., wearing the team uniforms. Some of the more "respectable" townfolk must have thought this was carrying sexual equality just a bit too far indeed!

Toronto-born Johnny Coulon won the world bantamweight title in 1910. During the war he taught boxing in the U.S. army.

34

From around the turn of the century Canadian football began to change, gradually abandoning the "flow" of British rugby and adopting the "stop and start" style of American football. In 1911, when McGill named Notre Dame's Frank Shaughnessy as coach, many regarded the move as a sell-out of Canadian sport. This photo of a game between McGill and U of T shows the original "Big Train," Smirle Lawson of Varsity, heading for a touchdown.

Boxing fans, almost all of them wearing sporty "boaters," encircled the makeshift ring to watch the opening-night bout at Toronto's Christie Pits.

Are these jail-birds, posing with their warden, or are the stripes there to slim down the figures of the Fatmen's baseball team of Fernie, B.C.?

Fred "Cyclone" Taylor left the famed Renfrew Millionaires in 1911 to lead Vancouver to its first Stanley Cup win. In 1915, in 126 games he scored 148 goals!

trainers ran horses under false names; jockeys were frequently paid more money to lose than to win races. It got so bad that the sport was banned in all but a handful of American states. In 1910 the Canadian parliament ruled bookies off the tracks and substituted pari-mutuel betting, administered by the jockey clubs, which turned out to be the salvation of the "sport of Kings" in the Dominion.

a line-up of habitant stars

The sport, of course, was hockey. Every town, village and crossroads had an amateur team of some sort, but the trend was clearly towards professionalism. On the evening of January 5, 1910, the National Hockey Association (the fore-runner of the National Hockey League) launched its inaugural season before 3,000 fans in a small, noisy firetrap called the Jubilee Rink in Montreal. The occasion also marked the debut of the famed "Flying Frenchmen," the Montreal Canadiens.

The NHA was formed following a disagreement among owners of teams in the professional Eastern Canada Hockey Association, and included the Montreal Wanderers, who defected from the older league, the powerful Renfrew Millionaires, and teams from Cobalt and Haileybury in Ontario's booming mining belt. The new league was well bankrolled. A.J. O'Brien, owner of the Renfrew franchise, was offering unheard-of salaries up to $3,000 a season to lure star players like Lester Patrick and Fred Whitcroft from western Canada to play for his team.

The suggestion was made that an all-French-Canadian team would draw well in Montreal, and Jack Laviolette was hired to recruit a line-up of habitant stars. Before long he had signed such great Quebec players as "Newsy" Lalonde, Didier Pitre and Joe Cattarinich, and the *bleu, blanc et rouge* of the Canadiens was ready to take to the ice for the first time. Shortly afterward, a slender, sad-faced, seemingly emotionless young goalkeeper named Georges Vezina, soon to be known across Canada as "the Chicoutimi Cucumber," perhaps the greatest netminder ever to stand between the pipes, was added to the roster. Although the Canadiens finished in last place that first season, one of the greatest dynasties in the history of Canadian hockey had been born . . . a dynasty based partially on the unique NHA provision that the Montreal team would enjoy the right of first refusal over all French-speaking players emerging from the amateur ranks.

The new league was a success from the outset. The Shamrocks and Canadiens drew well in Montreal. The Renfrew Millionaires, with the most powerful team that money could buy, packed their rink for every home game. Some of the wildest games in the history of Canadian sports took place in the raw, icy cold, silver- and gold-rich towns of Cobalt and Haileybury. On the Ontario mining frontier money was a cheap commodity, and huge bets were made in support of the local heroes. Afterward fights would continue in the bars and saloons and along the main streets in thirty- and forty-below temperatures into the chill January and February dawns.

"he was tough!"

Each NHA team had at least one superstar. Renfrew's "Cyclone" Taylor, the first to wear pads when he obtained some pieces of felt from a livery stable and had them sewn into the shoulders of his jersey, was the idol of thousands of fans, and a future charter member of the Hockey Hall of Fame. "Newsy" Lalonde, a native of Cornwall, Ontario, averaged a goal a game, and was one of the greatest French Canadian athletes of all time. Lester Patrick has become a legend. Without a

doubt, one of the roughest, meanest hockey players ever to lace on skates was Sprague Cleghorn, also of the Renfrew Millionaires. Cleghorn was just plain mean; he would have tripped his grandmother into the end-boards if she were in position to score a goal against his team. Once, while sitting out a leg injury, he was arrested for beating up his wife with a crutch. King Clancy, who played against him at a much later date, said of the Renfrew forward: "He was just a terrible man to play against . . . an absolute master with the butt-end. Holy mackerel, he was tough!"

the first artificial ice arenas

In those days games were played on natural ice which was scraped between periods but could not be reflooded so that it gradually deteriorated as the game continued. The season usually ran from the beginning of the year to early March. After that the warming sun made it hard to keep ice in the rinks, and more than one championship game was played on a cushion of slush covered with pools of water.

In 1912 Lester Patrick and his brother Frank deserted the National Hockey Association to help launch a new professional league on the west coast, using the country's first artificial ice arenas in Vancouver and Victoria. This innovation, almost immediately adopted in eastern Canada, meant that the season could be extended as long as desirable. At about the same time the position of rover was eliminated, reducing the number of players from seven to six. Other rule changes were made to speed up the game.

In hockey, as in so many other things, a new era was at hand – an era that would be better in some ways, not as good in others, but certainly different from what had gone before.

An item in the sporting pages the other day alluded to the fact that one "Newsy" Lalonde had "signed up" with some club or other to play hockey for the winter. "Newsy" Lalonde is but one out of many, and we do not wish to single him out for special criticism, but it would appear to most of us, that if these young gentlemen are doing any "signing up" at the present juncture, it should be with the Department of Militia to serve their Team and Country. Professional hockey can well be dispensed with at a time when recruiting officers are scouring the country for able-bodied young men who would make tough soldiers, and it is very nauseous to see the promoters of various hockey clubs bartering in cash for the services of men to stay home and confine their exhibitions of prowess to the ice.

Shortly after the outbreak of war, Saturday Night *printed this vitriolic editorial denouncing professional hockey players as service evaders.*

CHAPTER THREE

Boom to Bust

Quoth Uncle Sam, "I hate to see
Them Canucks get the draw on me.
I'll hike to Ottawa," says he,
"And coax for reciproci-tea."

Advertisement for Red Feather Tea, circa 1911.

When a cold Ottawa dawn greeted New Year's Day, 1911, Wilfrid Laurier had been prime minister of Canada for almost fifteen years. Outwardly, he seemed secure in office.

About to enter his seventieth year, the prime minister exhibited the energy and enjoyed the good health of a much younger man. Always well groomed and impeccably dressed, with his perfectly fitted waistcoats, frock coats and striped trousers, with his tall hats and jewelled cravats, Laurier continued to be one of the most striking figures ever to grace the Hill.

He was usually eloquent, and at times a fiery speaker. His triumph at Queen Victoria's Diamond Jubilee in London some years earlier, when he had emerged as the premier premier of Britain's self-governing colonies, had earned him a knighthood and the admiration of his countrymen.

A Canadien whose ancestors had emigrated to the New World less than forty years after Champlain, he had done much to heal the wounds between English and French, and the country seemed unified.

The nation was enjoying a period of unprece-dented growth and prosperity. A spirit of optimism prevailed, and the outlook was bullish from Atlantic to Pacific. The flow of immigrants from the Old World continued, and was reaching flood-tide proportions. There was a wheat boom across the prairies, a lumber boom in the rain forests of the west coast, a mining and industrial boom in Ontario, a pulpwood boom in Quebec, even a steel and coal boom in Nova Scotia. Everywhere railways were a-building – not just one new transcontinental line, but two, the Canadian Northern and the National Transcontinental, plus dozens and dozens of local, just slightly less ambitious projects. Most spectacularly of all, especially in the new West, there was a wildly speculative real estate boom; in a country which had more unoccupied square miles of territory than any other on earth, the price of land was escalating far beyond the perimeters of healthy, common sense. In the spirit of the times, however, it seemed a justifiable expression of confidence in the young country.

And so, when he arose on that chilly first day of January in 1911, Sir Wilfrid had every reason to look forward to yet another year at the helm of the still-young nation. But before many weeks passed, events were to come to a head which, in unlikely and uneasy combination, would change all that.

There was the question of reciprocity with the United States – an arrangement to lower tariffs

Wilfrid Laurier is featured on this fold-out brochure for "Psychine – Canada's Greatest Medicine." Ailments such as speaker's sore throat, night sweats, weak voice and decline were "instantly cured." (No evidence exists that the PM ever touched a drop.)

Opposite page: *An experimental farm float advertises Canada as "the land of milk and honey" and wheat and...*

LIBMAN, CH., Cloakmaker	12	49	ליבמאן יחיאל קלאוקמייקער
LEVY, P., Insurance Agent	16	50	לויו פ. אינשורענס אגענט
MATENKO, I., Teacher	23	65	מאטענקא יצחק לערער
MUROFCHICK, M., Merchant	7	74	מוראפטשיק מ. ביזנעסמאן
MARIN, M., Manufacturer	4	57	מארין מ. מאנופעקטשורער
MOROSHNICK, M., Druggist	9	78	מאראשניק מ. דראגיסט
MANSON, M., Hatmaker	18	44	מענסאן מאקס העטמעקער
NATHENSON, BENZION, Teach.	30	37	נאטהאנסאן בן ציון לערער
NOODELMAN, A., Cloakmaker	12	14	נאדעלמאן א. קלאוקמייקער
NISNEWITCH, A., Manufacturer	7	82	ניסנעוויץ א. מאנופעקטשורער
SOLOMON, S., Manufacturer	9	28	סאלאמאן ס. מאנופעקטשורער
SOLOMON, C. H., Manufacturer	92		סאלאמאן ס ה מאנופעקטשורער
SOLWAY, MINNIE, Shapiro	14	76	סאלוויי מיני שאפירא
SAPERO, K. L., Merchant	5	58	סאפערא ק.ל. ביזנעסמאן
STONE, B., Manufacturer	15	26	סטאון ב. מאנופעקטשורער
SINGEL, ?, J. J.	13	58	סינגעל טאס. י. י.
SINGER, J., Lawyer	23	22	סינגער דזש. לאיער
SINGER, L. M., Lawyer	26	43	סינגער ל. לאיער
SAMUEL, M., Skirtmaker	11	57	סעמיל מ. סקורט מייקער
SAMUELS, S., Cloakmaker	11	25	סעמילס ס. קלאוקמייקער
SOOOLKO, M., Mechanic	60	5	סקולקא מ. מעקעניק
ELLENBERG, M., Merchant	8	81	עלענבערג מ. ביזנעסמאן
EPSTEIN, S., Barber	11	16	עפשטיין ס. בארבער
POLLOCK, DR. M. A., Physician	23	77	פאלאק דר מ. א. פיזישען
PASTERNACK, C., Merchant	16	25	פאסטערנאק ח. ביזנעסמאן
PIVNICK, DR. M., Dentist	17	53	פיוניק דר מ. דענטיסט
FEINBERG, L., Merchant	9	39	פיינבערג לייבל ביזנעסמאן
FACTOR, S., Lawyer	17	08	פעקטאר ס. לאיער
FRIMAN, I., Merchant	12	19	פרימאן ישראל ביזנעסמאן
FRUMHARTZ, F., Printer	10	29	פרומהארץ פ. דרוקער
FRANKEL, E., Hatmaker	12	80	פרענקעל אליעזר העטמעקער
COHEN, A., Lawyer	15	99	קאהן אב. לאיער
KOLDOFSKY, FANNIE	12	70	קאלדאפסקי פייגל
KOLDOFSKY, S., Organizer	27	7	קאלדאפסקי שמשון ארגאנייזער
KOMINKER, A., Merchant	7	24	קאמינקער א. ביזנעסמאן
KONIKOFF, H., Cloakmaker	10	62	קאניקאף ה. קלאוקמייקער
KURTZ, R., Manufacturer	7	66	קורץ ראבל מאנופעקטשורער
KIRSHENBAUM, H. M., Jour'st	22	38	קירשענבוים ה. מ. זשורנאליסט
KIRSHNER, A., Cloakmaker	11	92	קירשנער א. קלאוקמייקער
KERTZER, D., Merchant	5	77	קירצער ד. ביזנעסמאן
CLAVIR, HARRY, Manufacturer	11	87	קלאוויר העלי ביזנעסמאן
KAMIN, J., Carpenter	9	20	קעמין דזש. קארפענטער
KAMIN, M., Presser	8	97	קעמין מ. פרעסער
KESSNER, W., Photographer	9	75	קעסנער וו. פאטאגראפער
KRONICK, S., Manufacturer	11	53	קראניק סעם מאנופעקטשורער
KRUGER, H., Cloakmaker	15	28	קרוגער ה. קלאוקמייקער
ROGUL, S., Merchant	8	25	ראגאל ס. ביזנעסמאן
ROSENBERG, L., Secretary	24	37	ראזענבערג ל. סעקרעטאר
ROSEN, M., Manufacturer	8	41	ראזען מ. מאנופעקטשורער
ROSENBAUM, T., Shochet	8	22	ראזענבאם תנחום שוחט
ROSENBLOOM, D., Organizer	17	02	ראזענבלום ד. ארגאנייזער
ROSS, S. M., Merchant	7	12	ראס ס. מ. ביזנעסמאן
RUBINOFF, I., Wholesaler	11	69	רובינאף י. האלסעלער
RHINEWINE, A., Journalist	24	21	ריינוויין א. זשורנאליסט
RIBY, A., Cloakmaker	11	96	ריבי א. קלאוקמייקער
SHAPIRO, S. M., Journalist	20	66	שאפירא שמואל מאיר זשורנאליסט
SHAPIRO, M., Merchant	6	75	שאפירא מאיר ביזנעסמאן
SHAPIRO, M., Insurance	14	03	שאפירא שמואל אינשורענס אגענט
SCHWARTZ, DR. M., Dentist	20	57	שווארץ דר מ. דענטיסט
SHULMAN, P., Lawyer	17	68	שולמאן פ. לאיער
STEIN, D., Tailor	14	09	שטיין דוד שניידער
STEIN, M., Merchant	7	74	שטיין מאיר ביזנעסמאן
SCHIFF, K., Manufacturer	9	69	שיף קלמן מאנופעקטשורער
SHER, A., Insurance Act	16	01	שעהר אברהם אינשורענס אגענט
SPIER, BENZION, Merchant	13	17	שפייער בן ציון ביזנעסמאן

This excerpt from a bilingual voters' list of 1919 gives a bird's-eye view of immigrant life in the Kensington Market Jewish ghetto of Toronto.

which would let primary products (specifically wheat) flow south at high prices, in exchange for giving Americans a better chance to sell manufactured goods in Canada. Westerners were particularly enthusiastic at the prospect of higher prices and lower costs. Naturally, eastern Canadian manufacturers opposed any such measure, appealing to Canadian patriotism by suggesting that economic accord would be but a prelude to political takeover. This fear was given some credence by the remarks of some influential Americans. "Canadian annexation is the logical conclusion to reciprocity" one American senator had said. "I hope to see the day when the American flag will float over every square foot of the British North American possesions," Champ Clark, Speaker of the American House of Representatives, declared in Washington.

Yet Laurier had come to believe in a measure of reciprocity, and his minister of finance would soon propose legislation to that end. The move was destined to alienate many of the prime minister's most influential supporters – including the chairman of the Toronto Board of Trade, the president of the Bank of Commerce and Clifford Sifton, the voice of western Liberalism.

the security of the empire

From another quarter came a second challenge. For several years there had been growing concern that the build-up of German sea-power, if not matched, might soon challenge Great Britain's naval supremacy and the security of the empire. Were Canada and the other self-governing dominions prepared to support the Mother Country? And how?

In the best tradition of Canadian politics, Laurier had hammered out a compromise in 1910 between those who thought Canada should do nothing and those who wanted to spend money on battleships for Britain. Canada would create her own navy. To placate those imperialists who believed in unstinting support for king and empire, it would be placed at the disposal of the British Admiralty in times of crisis; to reassure Canadian nationalists, the decision as to when such a step should be taken would rest not in London, but in Ottawa.

Laurier was probably justified in thinking that his solution would be acceptable to almost all shades of Canadian opinion; but, as the future was to disclose, it satisfied practically no one – involving too great a commitment for some, and not enough for others.

a "tin-pot" Canadian navy

In the following months Laurier faced two principal foes.

Robert Laird Borden, a Nova Scotia lawyer, had led the Conservative party without notable success for a full decade. A quiet, almost austere man with a thick moustache and neatly-parted, white hair, he had been a capable leader of the Opposition, though generally appearing bland in contrast to Laurier's flare and style in the House of Commons. Although he had originally endorsed Laurier's naval policy, Borden came to feel that the seriousness of the mounting German threat called for a direct contribution of ships or money to London, rather than the creation of a token, "tin-pot" Canadian navy. Laurier's Naval Bill was passed over his opposition, but Borden won supporters in several sectors by his stand.

And Borden, with the support of Sifton and other Liberals who had deserted Laurier, came out strongly against the government's proposal for reciprocity with the United States.

Laurier's second antagonist was as different from Borden as can be imagined. Strikingly handsome, dashing, elegantly dressed, Henri Bourassa would never go unnoticed in a crowd. With his

The decade saw a continuation of the flood of immigrants bound for the "Last, Best West." Families, like this Ukrainian couple and their six children, were housed at Quebec's immigration sheds to wait for the next CPR train to the Prairies. Few of them could afford the luxury of the 25¢ meal advertised on the station placard.

Henri Bourassa
Le Nationaliste

Nationalist, matchless orator, public watch-dog for Quebec, journalist and politician, Henri Bourassa was born in Montreal in 1868, a grandson of Louis-Joseph Papineau, the "rebel." He began his career in newspapers in 1910 as founder of the *Le Devoir*, the daily which during his years of control became the major political voice in Quebec. In 1899 he broke with his one-time mentor, PM Laurier, over sending troops to fight in the Boer War. In 1917, when the country was called to supply men again for an overseas war, Bourassa trumpeted, "Canada has done enough!" One of the most influential and scrupulous politicians of the time, when he stalked out of Commons Laurier quipped, "We need men like you in Ottawa . . . though I would not want two." Among his many writings, *Hier Aujourd'hui et Demain* (1916) stands out as a candid commentary.

flashing, dark eyes, he was a dramatic and compelling speaker, and an effective and prolific writer. With his recently founded Montreal newspaper *Le Devoir*, he usually expressed, and was often influential in formulating, the majority opinions of his fellow Canadiens from the province of Quebec.

He, too, opposed both Laurier's Naval Bill and reciprocity with the United States. But on entirely different grounds than Borden. Bourassa was both a Canadian nationalist *and* a Quebec nationalist, and his cause was to keep his country and his people free from domination by either the English or the Americans. For him, the Naval Bill offered too much to the one, and reciprocity proffered too much to the other.

The debate over these two contentious issues continued through that winter and spring and into the summer – not only in Ottawa but across the country. Finally Laurier decided to go to the people, the majority of whom he felt were behind him, especially on the issue of reciprocity.

crowds await election bulletins

The general election was set for the first day of fall – September 21, 1911. It was a day of sunshine in most parts of the country, although the chill of early autumn was unmistakably in the air. As night stretched from the Maritimes across Quebec, Ontario, the Prairies, and finally to British Columbia, crowds gathered in front of newspaper offices to read the bulletins summarizing the results from province after province.

Radio was still in the future and the only way of transmitting election results or other important information quickly was by telegraph. By means of their wire services, the newspapers were hooked up with all parts of the country. When important news was expected – when war was imminent, when a king or queen was mortally ill, or on election nights – the latest available information would be scrawled across sheets of newsprint and posted in the windows of the newspaper offices. As each fresh bulletin was pasted up, those on the inner perimeter of the crowd would press eagerly forward, and pass back the news to those who swarmed behind.

the wheat booms

Gradually the picture acquired focus – and what it showed surprised a great many people. By the time dusk settled over Vancouver and Victoria Laurier and his Liberals were out. The final returns gave Borden's Conservatives 134 seats to the Liberals' 87 – the exact opposite of the pre-election balance of power in the House of Commons. Somewhat unexpectedly Robert Laird Borden became the new prime minister of Canada.

On the surface it seemed a particularly opportune time to assume that responsibility. Across the great land the word for the economic situation continued to be "boom." Immigration, particularly to the west, continued unabated. In Saskatchewan wheat acreage increased from 1,130,084 acres in 1905 to 6,003,522 acres by 1914. Along the railroad lines spider-webbing across the prairies, instant towns and cities sprang up, complete with grain elevators, merchants, professional men, preachers and swindlers – all prospering from the wheat boom created by the sod-busting farmers – places with names like Elbow, Outlook, Pilot Mound, Rapid City, Baden, Mafeking, Onward and Stalwart. You had to be a drunkard or an incompetent or a plain, damn fool not to make a good living out of grain – one way or another.

In the larger urban communities in the West real-estate values continued to climb.

Optimism was unrestrained. Fort George, at the end of the Cariboo Trail, was heralded as the probable future capital of British Columbia. Local boosters and get-rich-quick artists insisted that no less than ten different railroads were either being built or in the planning stage, to link that budding metropolis with the eager outside world. By 1912 tiny town-lots, 50 feet by 100 feet, were going for $10,000.

Kamloops was being advertised in eastern Canada, Europe, and the United States as "the future Los Angeles of Canada." In downtown Edmonton property fronting on Jasper Avenue was commanding prices up to $10,000 *per foot.* In Calgary, where the first Stampede was held in the summer of 1912, a single lot at the corner of 7th Avenue and 2nd Street was offered at $300,000.

almost full employment

Around every western city, most towns, and even a few pin-point villages, subdivisions were surveyed and staked out in the surrounding wilderness or prairie – complete (on the maps) with street names, schools, churches, parks, hospitals and industrial complexes.

Prices escalated to dizzy heights – and took off from there. It seemed that almost everyone was speculating in land, and making money.

In industrial Ontario and Quebec the western boom brought healthy profit-and-loss statements and almost full employment (although wages remained low and hours long). Only the Maritimes failed to share in the good times to any real extent. The great majority of the immigrants pouring into the country passed through Halifax, but they hurried on west and left little there except their ties with the past, their seasickness, and a few infants and old people who had died in passage.

Nevertheless, Borden's government had its full share of problems. While unwilling to implement Laurier's Naval Bill, the new prime minister encountered widespread opposition to his proposed alternative – a direct contribution of $35 million to build three battleships for the Royal Navy. He

Real Estate

Real estate! was the magic word before the war west of Winnipeg, and now that there were two transcontinental railways running the breadth of the country, any farmer, speculator or businessman with the gambling urge could invest his dollars in the future of a hundred unknown prairie towns. Magazine ads like these were no help at all. The Homesteading Act laid down rules, but they applied only to federal land reserves. Would Medicine Hat, Fort George or Edmonton be the next big city?

MEDICINE HAT

In this, the future manufacturing centre and largest milling point in Western Canada, we have lots for sale ¼ of a mile from large manufacturing plants now in operation. Every lot is guaranteed to be dry and level.

WRITE NOW FOR PARTICULARS AND PRICES. VALUES WILL ADVANCE MORE RAPIDLY IN MEDICINE HAT THIS YEAR THAN IN ANY OTHER CITY IN CANADA.

THE ANDERSON LAND CO.
226 Eighth Ave. E., CALGARY, ALTA.

Fort George

The Commercial Centre of British Columbia's Inland Empire

FORT GEORGE is the future Chicago of the Great Inland Empire of British Columbia.

It is the centre of a natural waterway system over 1,000 miles in extent.

FORT GEORGE will be the Railway Hub of Inland British Columbia. The topography of the country makes this inevitable.

FORT GEORGE is the Gateway of the Great Peace River district, about which the whole world is talking.

Fort George spells great prosperity to those who invest their dollars in the wonderful destiny of this commercial centre of a mighty country.

Here is an opportunity of making your future prosperity assured—invest to-day.

Send for full particulars, terms, etc. We have 241 acres just one mile from Fort George post office.

WRITE US TO-DAY.

WIERS-THOMPSON 5 Thompson Block **Windsor, Ont.**

The Governor and Company of Adventurers of England trading into Hudson's Bay,

Incorporated A.D. 1670, COMMONLY CALLED

THE HUDSON'S BAY COMPANY

Will offer for sale

About 1,300 Business and Residential Lots centrally located in the City of

EDMONTON
ALBERTA

within The Hudson's Bay Reserve.

The Sale will be held at Edmonton May 14, 15, 16, 17. 18, 1912.

Edmonton is now served by three Transcontinental Railroads.

J. THOMSON
Winnipeg, Manitoba.

HUDSON'S BAY COMPANY'S OFFICES
McGill Street, Montreal.

SYNOPSIS OF CANADIAN NORTH-WEST

HOMESTEAD REGULATIONS

ANY even numbered section of Dominion Lands in Manitoba. Saskatchewan and Alberta, excepting 8 and 26 not reserved, may be homesteaded by any person who is the sole head of a family, or any male over 18 years of age, to the extent of one-quarter section of 160 acres, more or less.

Entry must be made personally at the local land office for the district in which the land is situate.

The homesteader is required to perform the conditions connected therewith under one of the following plans:

(1) At least six months' residence upon and cultivation of the land in each year for three years.

(2) If the father (or mother, if the father is deceased) of the homesteader, resides upon a farm in the vicinity of the land entered for, the requirements as to residence may be satisfied by such person residing with the father or mother.

(3) If the settler has his permanent residence upon farming land owned by him in the vicinity of his homestead, the requirements as to residence may be satisfied by residence upon the said land.

Six months' notice in writing should be given to the Commissioner of Dominion Lands at Ottawa of intention to apply for patent.

W. W. CORY
Deputy of the Minister of the Interior.

N.B.—Unauthorized publication of this advertisement will not be paid for.

Study Your 1913 Investments

Have You Invested in Real Estate, Bonds or Stocks?
Are You Interested in Canadian Industrial De-
velopment and General Business Conditions?
Are You Watching the Money-Market?

The

Financial Post
of Canada

Is read from coast to coast by successful Investors, Business and
Financial Men who require a weekly digest of the important de-
velopments in Canadian Investments and Conditions. The Post is
Concise in Form, Independent in Policy and National in Scope.

The service of the Post's Investor's Information Bureau is
free to Subscribers. Questions regarding financial matters are
answered by special letter.

WRITE FOR SAMPLE COPY
PUBLISHED IN TORONTO, SATURDAYS
$3.00 PER ANNUM

The Financial Post of Canada
"The Canadian Newspaper for Investors"
Montreal   Toronto   Winnipeg   Regina   Vancouver
London, Eng.   Chicago   New York   Paris, France

The economic barometer of the times, the Financial Post, *advertised itself as "a weekly digest of important developments in Canadian investments and conditions." And in 1913 their reading of the economic climate was excellent. By October 1913 financial wizards knew that the good years were over.*

finally managed to push it through the House of Commons under very acrimonious circumstances, only to see it defeated in the Senate. The result was that by 1914 Canada had no operative naval policy.

Borden also had to face charges of political corruption, particularly involving the building of the transcontinental Canadian Northern Railway, under the direction of William Mackenzie and Donald Mann. The fact that he had inherited this situation from his predecessor did not make it any easier for Borden to live with it politically. The promoters of the Canadian Northern had already been granted hundreds of millions of dollars worth of bond guarantees. Now they demanded more. Without further support, they said, the line would go bankrupt and the end-of-track would permanently remain at some unidentifiable point in the northern muskeg. Against a rising tide of opposition in the House of Commons and on editorial pages across the country, Borden saw no alternative but to provide them with an additional $45 million of public funds.

But the greatest threat to Borden's custodianship was the onset of a world-wide depression, which became more ominous throughout 1913, and hit over-extended Canada particularly hard.

In the space of a few months, "boom" turned to "bust." Wheat prices dropped dramatically. Unemployment increased in Ontario and Quebec.

Prices stayed high, and even rose, while buying power dwindled rapidly. Panic replaced confidence.

The bullish market in real estate dried up like bear droppings in an August heat wave. People scrambled to unload their holdings, almost always purchased on credit, but no one was buying. Ordinary men and women, caught short along with fly-by-night promoters, quick-buck agents and grasping politicians, saw their paper profits wiped out in not much more time than it takes a winter sun to set in northern Saskatchewan. Suddenly you couldn't give land away.

Many a western town's grandiloquent dreams of becoming a Canadian Chicago evaporated almost overnight, and some of those towns were soon to be erased from the maps, completely and forever. Many a street sign identifying "23rd Avenue" (where there had never, in fact, been even a 1st Avenue) was abandoned to the lonely, prairie winds and eventually to the drifting top soil of the ensuing years. One Hudson's Bay tract in Edmonton remained empty for forty years.

By early 1914 hard times lay heavy on the land. People were disillusioned. The great dream had somehow turned into a national nightmare. Many were without jobs. Some were actually threatened by starvation. And the government of Robert Laird Borden, like the country, was in very serious trouble.

The World of Stephen Leacock

The World of Stephen Leacock "Level-headed" Jefferson Thorpe, the barber; 280-lb. Joseph Smith, proprietor of the local hotel; the Rev. Dean Drone . . .who can forget the colourful characters that made up Stephen Leacock's Anytown, Canada–"Mariposa." Born in England in 1869, Leacock came to Canada at seven, grew up on farms near Lake Simcoe, Ontario, received his education at local one-room schoolhouses and Upper Canada College, and financed his university years by teaching. His first comic sketch appeared in the pages of *Grip* in 1894; his first book was a political science text; but it was his wit, satire and nonsense in books like *Sunshine Sketches* (1912) that won Stephen Leacock his reputation as one of the world's greatest humourists.

"When Mr. Smith took over the hotel, he simply put up the sign JOS. SMITH, PROP., and then stood underneath in the sunshine."

Chapter 1
The Hostelry of Mr. Smith

I DON'T know whether you know Mariposa. If not, it is of no consequence, for if you know Canada at all, you are probably well acquainted with a dozen towns just like it.

There it lies in the sunlight, sloping up from the little lake that spreads out at the foot of the hillside on which the town is built. There is a wharf beside the lake, and lying alongside of it a steamer that is tied to the wharf with two ropes of about the same size as they use on the Lusitania. The steamer goes nowhere in particular, for the lake is landlocked and there is no navigation for the Mariposa Belle except to "run trips" on the first of July and the Queen's Birthday, and to take excursions of the Knights of Pythias and the Sons of Temperance to and from the Local Option Townships.

In point of geography the lake is called Lake Wissanotti and the river running out of it the Ossawippi, just as the main street of Mariposa is called Missinaba Street and the county Missinaba

I   B

Chapter I, page 1 of Stephen Leacock's brilliantly funny chronicle of "Mariposa."

"His hair always seemed to need cutting . . . His clothes gave an effect of negligence."

Sketches of Rural Quebec

In 1914 a novel was published in Paris, France, written by a young French writer named Louis Hémon. No one knows whether the publisher knew at the time that its author was dead, killed by a train at Chapleau, Ontario. The novel was titled *Maria Chapdelaine*, and it told the story of a rural Quebec family trying to eke out a living near Péribonka, a town where Hémon had lived for a year. The book was an immediate success abroad; in Canada the response was mixed. Very few who read it seemed to think the novel was an accurate picture of

life in Canada, and passed it off as a romantic young writer's idyll. Whether the characters and conditions of the novel are representative of the real people and conditions in rural Quebec in 1913, we will never know for certain, but the chronicle that Louis Hémon left behind has become one of the best-loved and best-selling books ever written about Canada. These sketches (below and right) by Clarence Gagnon are part of a series of fifty-four miniatures by the Quebec artist, done to represent the everyday life of the Chapdelaine family.

" 'Make Land!' Rude phrase of the country, summing up in two words all the heart-breaking labour that transforms the incult woods . . . to smiling fields."

" . . . the candle flames wavered and shadows flitting across the face of the dead woman made her lips seem to be moving in prayer or softly telling secrets."

"The children all gathered about as a few drops of boiling syrup were allowed to fall upon the snow, where they instantly became crackly bubbles, deliciously cold."

Your Country Calls, *a 1915 painting by Paul Wickson of Paris, Ontario, shows a recruiting officer on horseback announcing the country's call to arms. Some farmers enlisted, others served the military effort by growing much needed grain and produce for those serving overseas.*

CHAPTER FOUR

War!

This war is like the suicide of civilization.

Prime Minister Robert Borden, 1915.

Civic holiday in 1914 fell on Monday, the third of August, and the long weekend was celebrated in the traditional way, with picnics, baseball games, regattas, steamboat excursions and dances. Across the country people caught fish, and scraped their knees, and burned their fingers, and laughed and cried, and fell in love, and listened to music, and read, and scolded children, and fell ill, and fell dead, much as they had always done.

Beyond the Atlantic, however, the captains and the kings were playing out the fateful, final moves in a dreadful chess game that would soon make normalcy only a fond memory.

The sequence of events which began with the assassination of the Archduke Francis Ferdinand in the obscure Balkan city of Sarajevo on June 28 built from crisis to crisis through the long, hot July days of 1914. Many Canadians followed these developments through their daily newspapers, but to the great majority they seemed remote and not of a nature to have any direct bearing on their lives.

On Tuesday, August 4, German troops began to move into Belgium. Twenty-four hours later Britain's ultimatum regarding Belgian neutrality expired, and No. 10 Downing Street issued a declaration that a state of war existed with Imperial Germany. In London that evening Sir Edward Grey, the British Foreign Secretary, told a friend: "The lamps are going out all over Europe. We shall not see them lit again in our lifetime."

And in Canada that evening, the six-inch headline on the front page of the *Toronto Star* said simply: "War!"

In 1914 Canadian ties with "the old country," the monarchy, and the empire were very close. School children received daily doses of Kipling, and filed to classes – boys through one entrance, girls by another – beneath reproductions of paintings of great British naval and military victories. Victoria Day (the late Queen's May 24 birthday) was celebrated with at least as much enthusiasm as July 1. The day-to-day news from Britain was often reported more fully in Canadian newspapers than whatever was happening in Ottawa, Montreal, Toronto, Winnipeg or Vancouver. The fleet exercises of the Royal Navy were covered in great detail. United Kingdom cricket and soccer results were assumed to be of primary interest. British general elections, such as the two in 1910, commanded columns of space every day of the campaign.

Thus when news of the outbreak of hostilities spanned the Atlantic, the dreadful reality immediately struck home. Across the land, in cities and

Character certificates were documents familiar to 418, 052 Canadians overseas. Young men like Charles Shields became a number on a ledger when they signed up. Over 50,000 men became statistics in the death-tally of the long war.

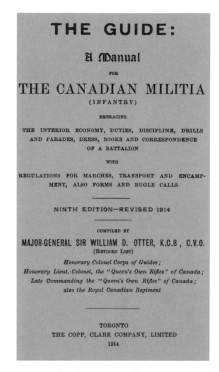

The ninth edition of William Otter's manual for the Canadian militia, first published in the previous century was standard issue to the raw recruit.

towns and villages, throngs gathered in the streets to share the burden of it. The *Toronto Globe's* description of the scene that was enacted on that city's Yonge Street could have been used to depict crowd reactions across the country:

For a moment the thousands stood still. Then a cheer broke. It was not for the war, but for the King, Britain, and – please God – victory. Toronto is British and its reception of the most sensational news in the history of the city was British. . . . Heads were bowed and the crowd began to sing "God Save the King". . . . [Then] the Queen City citizens joined lustily in that old song, "Britannia Rules the Waves" . . .

Newspaper editors and writers were virtually of one voice in assuming and endorsing Canadian participation in the war.

"In such an indisputable emergency, the duty of the hour for Canada can surely be no matter of doubt," said the *Halifax Herald.*

"We are committed to the work, and whatever is before us we will face with determination and courage, with every effort at our command and every resource," echoed the Peterborough *Examiner.*

presentiments of horrors

Politicians, of whatever region and stamp, were almost as unanimous. Laurier was on record as having said that, "when Great Britain is at war, Canada is at war." Even Henri Bourassa, the often strident spokesman for French Quebec, acknowledged that it was Canada's duty "to contribute within the bounds of her strength, and by means which are proper to herself, to the triumph, and especially to the endurance, of the combined efforts of France and England." Crowds in Montreal streets had sung "La Marseillaise."

Canadian newspapers were guardedly uncertain as to what the war would be like. Some, like the Halifax *Herald,* hoped that the modern rules of international conflict, as defined by the Geneva Convention, might lead to "due restraint" from barbarism. But a majority shared presentiments that the conflict would involve horrors beyond any previously known to man. "Armageddon" was a frequently used reference. One editor wrote that it would be the most terrible blood-bath since the fall of the Roman Empire; another that it would "set civilization back a thousand years."

a spirit of high adventure

Most average Canadians were not much concerned with such intellectual and philosophical musings. The mother country was at war, so Canada was at war – that's all there was to it. Every able-bodied Canadian male was expected to do his part, to join the colours, to serve king and country. Patriotism was rampant. The great majority of the youths and men of military age, at least in English Canada, simply assumed that they would be expected to enlist. And they were eager to do so, for they were familiar with only the glory of war, not the death. A fair number of them in that depression year were also eager for the free room and board the army offered.

In cities and towns in every province, men and boys lined up at armouries and hastily established mobilization depots. A spirit of high adventure, buoyed by a sense of camaraderie, prevailed. The common, popular conviction was that the despicable "Hun" (soon to be portrayed in recruiting posters as bayonetting infants and raping innocent women) would be crushed within weeks – at the most within a few short months. Those fortunate enough to get overseas would be home by Christmas, laden down with medals, to accept the bountiful homage of a grateful nation. "It'll probably all be over before I can get in on the fun," a new recruit in the Prince of Wales Regiment lamented to his fiancée.

Never fear; it would not be over for a long, long time.

No one could then have anticipated the four years and more of horror that lay ahead.

In the summer of 1914 Canada had virtually no military tradition or experience. Apart from sending a small volunteer force to the Boer War in South Africa at the turn of the century, she had never been involved in overseas hostilities since becoming a nation almost half a century earlier.

"Canadians have been as remote from war as if they dwelt on a separate planet," the *Toronto Star* commented. "Even the profession of soldiering has ceased among us."

a dollar a day for privates

Schoolboys endured cadet training each spring, but this involved no more than marching in dusty school grounds, polishing brass buttons and learning how to roll puttees for the annual inspection.

At the outbreak of war Canada's "army" consisted of a mere 3,110 men in uniform. A majority were recent immigrants from the United Kingdom. The rate of pay was a dollar a day for privates.

In addition, 74,213 men had received a smattering of training as members of part-time local militia units. Such reserve service was generally regarded as a means of supplementing low wages, and recruits looked forward to the annual summer training camps as a lark and an expense-paid vacation. In the summer of 1910, at the personal expense of its Colonel and patron, Sir Henry Pellatt (the builder of Casa Loma), 670 members of Toronto's Queen's Own Regiment had been taken to England for six weeks of training. "Gala Six Weeks For Toronto's 600," the *Toronto Star* headed its account of their departure.

No one outside the naval recruiting station seems to be interested in the ball scores (upper left).

Toronto mayor Tommy Church leans against the car, wondering which young men in boaters will sign up.

First and second generation Russian Canadians wait for a final blessing from their priest outside the church at Grierson St. and Jasper Ave. in Edmonton. In October 1914, the First Canadian Division left for England for combat training.

PAY.

The daily pay for the several ranks and appointments in the ACTIVE MILITIA (Infantry) are as under.*

Lieutenant-Colonel	$5 00
Major	4 00
Paymaster	3 00
Adjutant (in addition to pay of rank)	0 50
Musketry Instructor (in addition to pay of rank)	0 50
Quarter-Master	3 00
Chaplains, (rank of Major)	4 00
" (rank of Captain)	3 00
Captain	3 00
Lieutenant	2 00
" (provisional)	1 50
Sergeant-Major (if a Warrant Officer)	1 75
" (not a Warrant Officer)	1 50
Band Master (if a Warrant Officer)	1 75
" (if acting)	1 50

*The rates of pay for the Permanent Force are somewhat different.

Daily pay to men in the active militia started at $5.00 for a lieutenant-colonel and dropped through the ranks to 75¢ for privates and military buglers.

If Canada had no naval policy at the outbreak of the war, neither did it have anything that could legitimately be called a navy. The only ships acquired as a result of Laurier's "tin pot" Naval Bill were two ancient cruisers, the HMCS *Rainbow* and the HMCS *Niobe,* purchased from Great Britain in 1910. One on each coast, three thousand or more miles apart, they were presumably to guard the Atlantic and Pacific approaches to the Dominion. Their contributions to the war effort, however, were more Gilbert and Sullivan than Nelson and Drake.

In Halifax the *Niobe* had been jetty-bound since piling up on Cape Sable in 1911. In September 1914, with as hastily assembled and motley a crew as ever manned a naval vessel, she somehow managed to struggle to sea. A few weeks later, after chronic engine trouble and the threatened collapse of one of her funnels, she limped back into port, there to remain, surrounded by an ever-widening sea of beer bottles, until she was towed away to the scrapyard shortly after the conclusion of the war.

On the west coast the *Rainbow* was engaged in an unusual incident, the purpose of which was to repulse, not the German Navy, but 376 Sikhs from the East India who, according to the Immigration Department, were attempting to enter the country illegally aboard a Japanese ship, the *Komagata Maru.* In this the *Rainbow* was ultimately successful, the unhappy Sikhs agreeing to sail for home after the Canadian government undertook, not very graciously, to replenish the ship's food supplies. That was in July and August 1914. A few weeks later the *Rainbow* received orders to sail from her base at Esquimalt and intercept two German pocket-battleships which were rumoured to be lurking off the coast of British Columbia,

H.M.S. Niobe, *flagship of Canada's "tin-pot navy." In 1914, she was expected to protect Canada's east coast against attack, but after one disastrous foray to sea, she limped back to Halifax, never to go to sea again.*

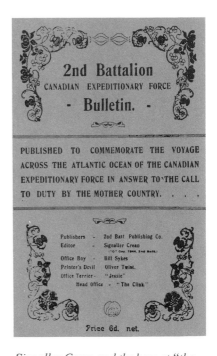

Signaller Crean and the boys at "the Clink" added a note of humour to this C.E.F. bulletin. The office terrier was probably on staff to keep the "printer's devil" at bay.

either of which could have sent her to the bottom with a single salvo. When she sailed, a message received from Ottawa was pinned up in her wardroom: "Remember Nelson And The British Navy. All Canada Is Watching." Fortunately for the *Rainbow* and her crew, she failed to locate the German dreadnoughts, if, indeed, they were ever in that vicinity.

For a few weeks in the summer of 1914, British Columbia had its own navy. Alarmed by rumours and aware of his province's vulnerability to German naval attack, the premier, Richard McBride, authorized the purchase of two submarines from a firm in Seattle, Washington. These vessels had been built to the specifications of the Chilean government which later had been either unable or unwilling to pay for them. McBride was therefore able to arrange a quick deal, and a purchase price of $1,150,000 was agreed upon. A cheque to that

amount was subsequently handed over to the shipbuilding firm (being delivered by the chief janitor of the British Columbia legislature, the only provincial "official" who happened to be free to make the trip to Seattle), and the west coast province had its "navy."

The submarines were shortly delivered to the Esquimalt Naval Base by employees of the builders, and placed under the command of one Lieutenant Keyes, late of the Royal Navy and a recent immigrant to Vancouver. Keyes and a few acquaintances who had had at least some experience with ships and seamanship, if not with submarines, left Vancouver by rail to accept delivery – Keyes acquiring some gold braid from a train conductor *en route* to add a touch of authority to the civilian blue serge suit he was wearing. Boarding the submarines upon arrival, he and his cohorts discovered that their already dim prospects of getting them to sea as fighting ships were further darkened by the fact that all of the operating instructions were printed in Spanish!

It was to the considerable relief of all hands, therefore, that the decision was subsequently taken to transfer ownership to the British Admiralty. By then the hysteria of imminent invasion had abated in British Columbia, and it was comfortably assumed that any such threat could be thwarted by the venerable *Rainbow*. Royal Navy records do not suggest that the two submarines played any significant roles in the subsequent war at sea.

"getting on with the job"

Meanwhile, most young Canadian males saw their contribution to lie in soldiering – in bearing arms to support king and country, the Dominion, the empire, the decency of womanhood, a way of life. From all quarters of Canada they flocked to the colours. But recruits who hurried to enlist in army units usually found that their enthusiasm was less than matched by the preparedness of the military authorities to receive them. Many of those who left factory jobs and harvest fields to become soldiers that fall were still drilling in civilian clothes and carrying broomsticks instead of rifles some months later. Experienced officers and drill instructors were in critically short supply. Everything needed to build an army was scarce.

Those who joined Winnipeg's 28th Canadian Infantry Battalion spent their first winter billeted in a cavernous old structure called the "Horse Show Building." In the absence of bunks, they slept as best they could on the sawdust and manure covering the floor of the arena. There was little heat, and temperatures often dropped to 30 and 40 degrees below zero at night. Toilet facilities consisted of a dozen outhouses for several hundred men, who had to line up in front of them on frigid January mornings. No provision whatever had

been made for off-duty recreation. Twice a day the men were marched over a mile in the darkness to a converted warehouse on Portage Avenue where a catering firm provided what passed for breakfast and supper.

While the commitment of most Canadians to the war was spontaneous and eager, the early stages of "getting on with the job" often involved moments of high comedy. The simple truth was that hardly anyone in Canada had any real knowledge of how a nation went about getting ready to fight a war.

One who did – or thought he did – was Colonel Sam Hughes, Borden's Minister of Militia and National Defence. Hughes, a vastly egotistical, frequently eccentric, and characteristically abrasive man, would shortly become the most controversial figure in the Canadian war effort. Already, in the summer of 1914, he was very much in the limelight. Within a few weeks of the outbreak of hostilities he had organized and set in operation a great training camp and staging area for Canadian troops at Valcartier, in the valley of the Jacques Cartier River, not far from Quebec City.

to fight and die as Canadians

As even his numerous enemies would concede, Valcartier was an impressive personal triumph for Sam Hughes. There, during that first September of the war, four miles of tents were erected. Troops poured in from all across the country. Countless tons of equipment were assembled. An artillery range was established. Dozens of cook houses were built. And, because the war would involve mounted cavalry and horse-drawn guns and vehicles, acres of corrals were erected across the plains and thousands of animals were shipped in aboard railway cattle-cars.

Hughes assumed personal, on-the-spot command of Valcartier. Seldom seeming to sleep, he

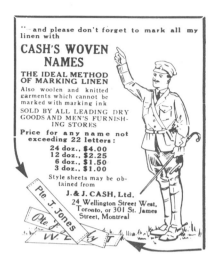

"...and please don't forget to mark all my linen with

CASH'S WOVEN NAMES

THE IDEAL METHOD OF MARKING LINEN

Also woolen and knitted garments which cannot be marked with marking ink

SOLD BY ALL LEADING DRY GOODS AND MEN'S FURNISHING STORES

Price for any name not exceeding 22 letters:

24 doz., $4.00
12 doz., $2.25
6 doz., $1.50
3 doz., $1.00

Style sheets may be obtained from

J. & J. CASH, Ltd.

24 Wellington Street West, Toronto, or 301 St. James Street, Montreal

Any well prepared enlisted man or officer should have his woolen and linen wardrobe marked with Cash's woven names. How could you go wrong with 24 dozen for $4.00? But who would need 24 dozen name tags?

was here, there, and everywhere, often embellishing his colonel's uniform with plumed hats, capes, swords and other colourful accoutrements when he carried out his incessant inspections. He took special pleasure in handing out on-the-spot promotions to officers who happened to gain his favour. On other occasions he could be crudely and grossly insulting to his peers and subordinates, and to visiting dignitaries and politicians alike.

Predictably, he insisted on directing the embarkation of the first Canadian contingent, which sailed from Quebec City, via Valcartier, on the first day of October, 1914.

Having seen "his boys" off, Hughes hurried on ahead of them on a fast oceanliner. Arriving in London, he discovered that the British War Office, under Lord Kitchener, planned to break up the Canadian regiments and place the men under more experienced British officers. Hughes protested.

"You have your orders," Kitchener told him. "Carry them out."

"I'll be damned if I will," Hughes replied, spinning on his heel and making his exit.

Hughes believed that Canadians should be allowed to fight and die together as integrated units, rather than be handed over to the Imperial high command, as colonials, to be dispersed as the British authorities might see fit. In this, he was on firm popular ground back home. The Canadians wanted to contribute, certainly, but as Canadians and not just as reserve soldiers of the British Empire. Hughes won his battle, although the jousting with the Imperial authorities would go on throughout the first half of the war.

Meanwhile the troops of the First Canadian Division impatiently waited out the boredom of their grey, autumn North Atlantic passage. Caught up in a spirit of shared adventure, they told each other that whatever lay ahead could scarcely be worse than the waiting and uncertainty.

In that naive belief they were terribly, tragically wrong.

As the war began to escalate in Europe, Canada hastily gathered together its first raw recruits at Valcartier, Quebec. The young men in this vast army of tents were the first to see the atrocities of war, and the first to give up their lives.

CHAPTER FIVE

Mud Bath, Blood Bath

The Canadians. . . undoubtedly saved the situation.

War Office communiqué on Battle of Ypres, 1915.

Early in 1915, after three miserable months of dampness, cold and boredom at a training camp on England's Salisbury Plain, the first Canadian troops began to move across the English Channel and into battle.

The struggle they joined had already settled into the pattern it would follow for the next four long years. By then any chance that might have existed for a quick, strategic victory by either side had been dissipated by the mutual hesitancy and ineptitude of the Allied and German high commands. Gone was any chance that it would be a short war.

The great armies faced each other in a terrible, almost hopeless stalemate, dug in along a looping line from the North Sea to Switzerland called "the western front." Until the final Allied breakthrough, late in 1918, that front would seldom waver more than a few hundred yards in either direction at any point. When the Canadians took their places in the front lines for the first time, the war had already become one of attrition, of mindless endurance, of stubborn survival – a war that could only be won by wearing down the enemy, until in the balance of casualties he could be outnumbered and finally overrun.

Meanwhile the same ground would be fought over continuously until no living, growing thing remained, nor a square yard of earth that hadn't been blasted and churned into terrible sterility. In the flat, featureless corridor between the trenches called "no man's land," barely perceptible ridges and mounds became vital military objectives, to be captured, lost and retaken – each time at the cost of thousands of dead and dismembered, maimed and missing. From its baptism of fire early in 1915 to the final weeks of hostilities, the entire Canadian army contested an area not much larger than three or four prairie townships.

It was, above all, a war of the trenches. Both sides constructed elaborate and intricate belowground networks, so similar in design that the soldiers of one could overrun and occupy the fortifications of the other with little sense of disorientation – apart from the different words used in official notices and under the pinned-up pictures of attractive females.

Front line trenches were dug as deep as local conditions permitted, usually until water began to seep in – which might be anywhere from two to six or even more feet. From them communication trenches zigzagged back to support lines and command stations, while others probed out in the opposite direction to provide observation posts within earshot of the enemy.

"Keep your mouth shut and don't talk to strangers!" is the message of this Canadian 4th Army Christmas card.

Opposite page: *The tortured landscape seems to swallow up crouching machine gunners. For these men the war meant a few muddy, bloody acres of land.*

In the trenches near Courcelette, France, army medics attend to the wounded. Canadian casualties there, from October 15, 1915 to September 3, 1916, were the heaviest up to that point in the war.

Generals and field marshals were unconscionably slow in realizing that the invention of the machine gun had fundamentally changed the nature of war, rendering cavalry obsolete and making any kind of frontal assault almost suicidal. And when they did realize it, they seemed abysmally incapable of devising new tactics to meet the changed circumstances. The result was that millions of men were sent to their deaths in often futile and always bloody attacks across open ground. The hated order to go "over the top" usually came at dawn. Between attacks there were long periods of boredom, underscored by the almost continuous thunder and lightning of the artillery and punctuated by the occasional whine of snipers' bullets.

no man's land

Other wars had seen armies locked in hand-to-hand combat, but never on such a colossal scale, and never for such an extended period. No man's land was seldom wider than a couple of city blocks, and frequently the lines were separated by as little as thirty yards. On Christmas Eve 1915, Canadian and German soldiers joined in singing "Silent Night" and other traditional carols, the two languages blending across the narrow strip of frosted, shell-torn ground. Although they seldom saw each other (except, perhaps, in final, deathly confrontation), men came to know the enemies they faced, day after day and month after month, by hearing their voices, and the little, ordinary sounds of life in the trenches – the laughs and grunts, the shuffling of feet, the coughs, the rattle of mess-kits. It was an intimacy bred not of fraternization or camaraderie (because the rule of survival was kill or be killed), but out of an awareness of common suffering and shared misery.

Seldom have human beings ever had to exist under more appalling conditions than those endured by the soldiers who manned the front lines. There was, of course, fear – although that was numbed after a time by the boredom and the fatigue and the sense of hopelessness. There were the moans and screams of the wounded. There was the horror of seeing friends maimed, blinded, turned into corpses. There was the general insanity of it all, and the particular reality of shell shock, the chronic concussion caused by the big guns, which temporarily destroyed men's minds and wills.

But, worse even than the constant threat of whole or partial death, was the wretchedness of life lived in such circumstances. Forced to grovel in the earth like animals, the men were constantly wet, cold, dirty. Boots and uniforms mildewed and fell apart. A man with a clean, dry pair of socks to put on was much to be envied. "Trench foot," a rotting of the flesh between and around the toes, was common. So was "trench mouth," a painful and highly contagious infection of the gums. Everybody had lice. There were the smells – of sweat and cordite and urine and fear and death. Rats as big and bold as alleycats ran through the trenches, and grew sleak and fat on the putrefaction.

the everlasting bully beef

And always the mud – a more real enemy, much of the time, than the Germans across the way, who had also to contend with it.

The soldiers slept where and when they could – sometimes in the ooze at the bottom of the trenches, sometimes in candlelit dug-outs just behind, often on their feet, slumped against walls and sandbags.

The meals were bleakly monotonous, providing minimal sustenance and no uplifting of spirits. The regular fare was the everlasting bully-beef, hard and sometimes wormy biscuits, jam that was half seeds and half turnip, an occasional stew of stringy meat and vegetables. Mercifully, there was usually a supply of hot tea.

The standard tour of duty in the front lines was three or four days, which was all a man could stand before collapsing physically and mentally. Relief provided a few precious hours behind the lines, a chance to sleep in a dry place, to bathe and shave, to eat a decent meal, to be partially restored before the time came to walk back into the battle.

determination to endure

Worst of all, there was no basis for hope, no reason to think that tomorrow or the day after would be any better than today or yesterday, no indication that there might ever be an end to it.

Incredibly, out of that almost total denial of everything that is human, there came countless acts of courage and self-sacrifice that were superhuman.

Incredibly, too – but also as a partial explanation of their determination to endure – the Canadian soldiers never lost their sense of humour, although it was often appropriately bitter. There was, for instance, the popular verse written by Corporal Cyril Brown, of Port Hope, Ontario:

Now here's a bit of shelter, boys, a cozy place to
    camp,
So kindly make yourselves at home, and if the
    feet be damp,
Keep on your socks and "Kitcheners," tuck in the
    blankets tight,
And pray you'll still be living this time tomorrow
    night.

The Canadian First Division took over four thousand yards of the front line before the ancient Flemish city of Ypres in mid-April 1915, relieving the Eleventh French Division. Their assignment: to stand fast in the face of expected German attacks, and specifically to hold a slight rise known as

This young ambulance driver was one of hundreds of anonymous women who worked in the Canadian Army Medical Corps, taxiing the wounded to field hospitals. Not all the heroes and casualties of the war were men.

Behind the Front Lines

Behind the front lines the war took on a dimension broader than just a struggle from shell hole to shell hole. For men and women in the medical corps, the war was one of bloodied linen, disease, bandages, gangrenous arms and legs that had to be amputated – and the anguish and death-cries of unknown soldiers who would never see their loved ones back home. For supply sergeants, the war at times meant a diminishing store of shells and the concern that what was critical to the next offensive would not be available. At the field post office cards, letters and packages piled up, some mailed three and four months before, many addressed to husbands, sons and brothers already buried in some mass grave. All outgoing mail had to be scrutinized and details of manoeuvres opaqued out. Behind the front lines food had to be grown, horses fed and watered, the dead buried, communiqués written, weapons repaired, teeth extracted, clothes mended, and shell-shocked men talked back from their private hell to sanity.

"This won't hurt a bit. . . " but it probably did anyway. These were the days of slow drills and no local anesthesia.

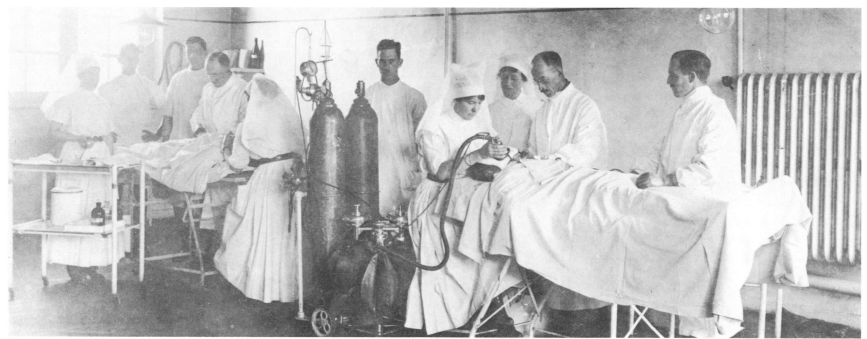

The nurse administers ether while the surgeon sews up the damage. Though clinically clean, field hospitals were usually poorly equipped, and doctors worked around the clock.

The quartermaster's stores at the front was not exactly a supermarket of variety: cartons of iron rations, tobacco and tins of meat the men called "dog food."

This "mobile" field post office could be mistaken for a Prairies immigrant's cart. Letters from home were often a soldier's only contact with Canada.

The battlefield near Vimy Ridge, the shell-torn site of the first major Canadian victory a year before (see p. 56), being ploughed before potatoes are planted in April 1918.

61

Gravenstafel Ridge, and a patch of shattered, skeletonized oak trees called St. Julien Wood.

The area had seen weeks of heavy fighting, and the sector of the front lines taken over by the Canadians was in terrible shape. The positions were ill-conceived, sloppily executed, badly maintained. The trenches, in some places only two or three feet deep, afforded only minimum protection. The usual sandbag breastworks were completely inadequate; there were only a few token strands of barbed wire; and no parados (earthworks to protect against shrapnel from shells falling to the rear) had been constructed. The ground was mud-slop, seemingly bottomless, and as clutching as quicksand. Then there was the stench and the filth. "The ground where the men stand is paved with rotting bodies and human excreta," a Canadian captain noted in his report.

During their first week at the front the Canadians encountered only light enemy action, although many of them came to know what it meant to see a comrade blown to bits or hideously wounded. And a sense of foreboding, of waiting for something ugly and unknown, hung over the front lines.

poison gas

April 22, 1915, was a sunny, benevolently warm, early spring day in Flanders. A lazy, still day, with the few puffs of white cloud seeming scarcely to move in the blue sky. There was only spasmodic, almost desultory firing between the lines.

By then the Canadians had been able to make their trenches somewhat more livable, and shortly after noon the Third Infantry called divisional headquarters with a request for some playing cards and a few mouth organs. The quartermaster regretted that he was out of playing cards, but sent up a case of harmonicas, and soon the strains of "Pack Up Your Troubles" began to drift out

across the barren wastes of no man's land.

Later in the afternoon a light breeze came up, blowing from the direction of the enemy trenches. Barely perceptible to the Canadians, it was enough to create a stir of activity in the German lines. Engineers were consulted, orders were given, and the valves of hundreds of sinister-looking metal canisters were opened. The long-rumoured use of poison gas became a reality on the western front.

barrage of the big guns

It came drifting toward the Canadian trenches, an evil-looking, dense, ground-hugging cloud, moving at five or six miles an hour. Some later remembered it as yellow, others as green – all as the colour of terror and death. The chlorine burned eyes and throats, destroyed lungs. Those enveloped by it choked, gagged, gasped, coughed, died. The French colonial troops on the Canadians' flank fled in panic.

Seizing their advantage, the Germans attacked in force. Outnumbered two to one, reeling from the gas, pounded by artillery fire, twenty-one Allied battalions (twelve of them Canadian) somehow rallied . . . and held.

That night, and the next day, and for two more weeks the enemy poured everything it had into the Ypres salient. There were several further tides of poison gas. The barrage of the big guns continued remorselessly, day and night. The German infantry came on, wave after wave.

The Canadians and their British empire comrades hung on. The decimated oak forest of St. Julien, by then renamed "Kitchener's Wood," was several times lost, and several times retaken. The Canadian 8th Battalion clung to Gravenstafel Ridge against all enemy efforts to overwhelm it.

By the end of the first week in May, when the front was eventually restabilized, the Canadians had suffered fearsome casualties – better than one

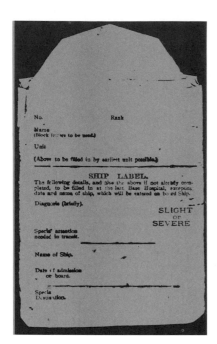

"Body labels" pinned to the wounded at the field ambulance or dressing station contained the soldier's papers. Overcrowded base hospitals tried to give priority to those who had been severely wounded. Almost 156,000 Canadian troops returned home wounded; another 2,000 never left the veterans' hospitals alive.

in five were listed as killed in action, missing, or wounded. The Tenth Battalion's strength had been reduced from 800 to 193, the Sixteenth had less than 250 still in the field, and other outfits like British Columbia's Gordon Highlanders and Regina's "Fighting Fifth" had been similarly hard hit.

The initiation at Ypres also revealed an Achilles' heel that was to plague the Canadian soldier for most of the first half of the war – the fact that he was supposed to fight with a gun that was quite likely not to work just when he needed it most. The Ross rifle, manufactured for the Canadian army by Scottish industrialist Charles Ross and enthusiastically endorsed by Sam Hughes, was unquestionably a splendid target rifle. In the close quarters and rapid-fire conditions of trench warfare, however, its finely tuned bolt and cartridge chamber had a tendency to seize up, making the weapon inoperable and leaving its owner frustrated and unable to defend himself. In the Ypres campaign thousands of Canadian infantrymen found themselves frantically trying to free jammed mechanisms in the face of enemy attack, and 1,452 of them angrily discarded their Ross rifles and replaced them with British Lee-Enfields, obtained in any way they could get them.

battle-tested Canadians

Throughout the remainder of 1915 and into the next year the opposing armies, including the now battle-tested Canadians, remained locked in a futile bloodbath which provided few victories, but exacted a ghastly toll in lives. Occasionally the stupefying sameness was broken by a savage battle – such as the struggle for "the Mound," near the ravished village of St. Eloi, in March and April of 1916. By then the Second and Third Canadian Divisions had joined the remnants of the First in the front lines. Again the soldiers of the Dominion fought with courage and distinction.

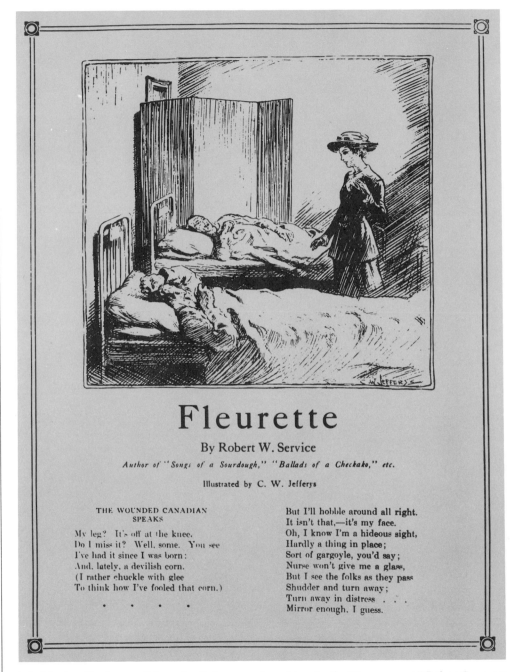

Fleurette

By Robert W. Service

Author of "Songs of a Sourdough," "Ballads of a Checkako," etc.

Illustrated by C. W. Jefferys

THE WOUNDED CANADIAN SPEAKS

My leg? It's off at the knee.
Do I miss it? Well, some. You see
I've had it since I was born:
And, lately, a devilish corn.
(I rather chuckle with glee
To think how I've fooled that corn.)

. . . . .

But I'll hobble around all right.
It isn't that,—it's my face.
Oh, I know I'm a hideous sight,
Hardly a thing in place;
Sort of gargoyle, you'd say;
Nurse won't give me a glass,
But I see the folks as they pass
Shudder and turn away;
Turn away in distress . . .
Mirror enough, I guess.

"As I had grabbed my stuff from the Yukon, now I would make the War my meat," Robert Service is alleged to have said after submitting his poetry collection, Rhymes of a Red Cross Man, *to his publisher in 1916. "Fleurette," a verse from the book, is an example of Service's popular but grim wit.*

Private Ross

Borrowed an Auto-Strop from his chum —he used it once and immediately wrote home for one.

Don't wait for a request from your soldier boy—include an AutoStrop in your next Overseas package.

Remember, that the AutoStrop is the only razor he can absolutely depend on—because of its self-stropping feature it is always ready for service.

Price $5.00
At leading stores everywhere

AutoStrop
Safety Razor Co.
Limited
83-87 Duke Street,
Toronto, Ont.

54 5 18

AutoStrop
SAFETY
RAZOR

Again the inadequacy of the Ross rifle proved a terrible handicap to proud and courageous fighting men.

History usually paints war in broad strokes, preserving the names of campaigns and battles, of generals and of diplomats, and reducing the rest to the impersonality of casualty statistics. Yet war can only be understood as the aggregate of thousands, perhaps millions, of individual experiences. Although surrounded by hordes of others, a soldier is entirely alone when he goes into battle for the first time, and he must live – or die – with whatever he brings to that moment, whatever his life and his luck have equipped him with, no more and no less. It was so on the western front.

The youngest son of a Saskatchewan wheat farmer, not yet out of his teens and just four months removed from his family and his best girl, stared at the headless body of a plumber's apprentice from Digby, Nova Scotia, who had become his friend. There were no tears in the eyes of the prairie youth. Not then.

A former star athlete from Vancouver, propped against the dirt wall of a dug-out just behind the lines, threw pebbles, bits of dried biscuits and anything else he could find to keep the rats from nibbling at the shattered, gangrenous stub of his leg.

A father of three from Hamilton, Ontario, a man who had never been lucky enough to have a steady job in civilian life, dug trenches in a cold, relentless rain. Every now and then he had to cut through the decomposing body of a weeks-dead French soldier. He vomited the first time it happened, but after a while he came to accept the fact that corpses were part of life on the western front; in fact they were easier to shovel than the thick, clinging mud.

What brought them there, these men and boys, to that strange place and that incredible mockery of life? Naive patriotism? A misguided thirst for adventure? The promise of three square meals a day? Whatever it was, it wasn't the prospect of easy money. Ordinary soldiers were paid a dollar a day. A totally disabled private could look forward to a pension of $12.50 a month. A dead private's widow would receive 30 cents a day, plus a dime a day for each of her first two children; larger families would simply have to slice the bread thinner and water the stew still further.

Yet, somehow the Canadian soldier managed to get the awful, absurd job done.

In the late summer of 1916 word came to move out of Flanders and join the great, general offensive planned for the Somme.

Behind were the bloody initiation rites; ahead lay many more battles, many more victories, many more dead to be listed.

Still to come were Verdun, Amiens, Valenciennes, Passchendaele, Epeny, Courcelette, Canal du Nord, Arleux, the Scarpe . . . and Vimy Ridge.

Canada at War

"...You follow up a plank road and then cut off over festering ground, walking on the tips of shell holes which are filled with dark unholy water. You pass over swamps on rotting duck boards, past bleached bones of horses with their harness still on, past crude crosses sticking up from the filth, and the stink of decay is flung over..."

from a letter to Arthur Lismer from Frederick Varley

Twenty-two-year-old Kenneth Forbes of Ottawa, a champion boxer in his school years was wounded in action twice before being transferred to the post of war artist.

65

Artists at the Front

Twenty years before colour photography, the only graphic records that depicted the war in living horror were the paintings done by artists commissioned by the War Records Office. Young Canadian painters, many working in small commercial and advertising companies, left their studios and were given the devastated landscapes and cities of Europe to paint. A.Y. Jackson, Frederick Varley and David Milne abandoned the colours and impressions of Canada for the starker realities of mud and blood and death in countries thousands of miles away from home. Representational painters Louis Keene, Arthur Nantel, Kenneth Forbes, Richard Jack (see p.2), and others experienced the same hardships as the regular soldier. Jackson was wounded in action; Nantel was captured in 1915 and spent the rest of the war as a prisoner; Keene spent the bitter winter of 1919 in Siberia. Of the best-known artists, only Tom Tomson (see pages 110-111), a pacifist, never painted the war at home or abroad.

Arthur Nantel spent over three years in a German prison camp, where he was one of the POWs he pictured above.

Born in Belgium, Alfred Bastien was attached to the 22nd Battalion of the Canadian Expeditionary Force. His Outpost, Neuville-Vitasse *catches a Canadian sentry on duty in the trenches.*

Louis Keene came to Canada in 1912 and worked as a cartoonist at the Montreal Herald *before enlisting in the machine-gun brigade. In 1919 he served with the Canadian contingent in Siberia (above) in the Allied effort at the end of the war to overthrow the Bolshevik government that had taken power in 1917.*

68

CHAPTER SIX

Keep the Homefires Burning

The Dominion Income War Tax Act, passed at the last session of Parliament, is now in force and all those liable must file the required returns....

Department of Finance, Ottawa, 1918.

Back in Canada people gradually adjusted to the drastically changed circumstances of their lives, and in time became almost used to them.

Yet the war could never be far from anyone's thoughts for very long. There were too many empty beds for that; too many absent husbands, sons, fathers, brothers, sweethearts; too many cruel, potentially final partings at railway stations, large and small, across the nation.

Those who stayed at home got behind "the boys overseas" in a great variety of ways. Many planted and tended victory gardens to supplement the food supply. Groups of women, from pampered debutantes to rough-handed farm housewives, met regularly to roll bandages. Others knitted gloves, sweaters and scarves in khaki-coloured wool. There were almost nightly card games, dances and other entertainments to send cigarettes and candy to the soldiers overseas. Workers pledged millions of dollars to buy Victory Bonds.

Patriotic rallies were held to encourage recruiting, which also received endorsement from almost every pulpit. In Toronto the T. Eaton Co. announced generous support of all employees who "joined the colours." In Edmonton the city council agreed to pay half-salary for the duration to all civic workers who enlisted, and granted free street railway transportation to those in uniform. Small towns like Fernie, British Columbia, conducted drives to purchase machine guns for local regiments. In Vancouver the Red Cross raised over $950,000 from private contributions. "War bread" made from inferior wheat and margarine (made from a variety of unsavoury oils and fats) were accepted with few complaints.

In a great many other ways daily life went on pretty much as usual. The stove still had to be fed in winter. The weekly wash still had to be done on Mondays. Kids still went to school. People who owned cottages managed to spend some time at them in the warm months. Most sports leagues continued to function, albeit with depleted team rosters and a dilution in the calibre of play. Women still had babies. Doctors still performed operations. Judges still heard cases. And there was, as always, a need for escape and amusement. The entertainment pages of the *Toronto Star* for May 1, 1916, for instance, advertised dancing at Sage & Co.'s new Luncheon and Tea Rooms; the opening of *Under Cover* starring Edward S. Robins, at the Royal Alexandra; and the Ernest Evans Circus, headlining the vaudeville bill at Lowe's Theatre. Edmonton audiences were thrilling to such silent movie stars as Charlie Chaplin,

The message of this Victory Bond drive handbill is clear and succinct. Women played a major role in home front campaigns to finance the war.

Opposite page: By 1917, over 35,000 women were employed in munitions in Ontario and Quebec. This interior view is by artist Henrietta Mabel May.

A Letter Home

Handsome in his uniform, young Gordon Gibson of Nelson, B.C., sat for his photo before being sent to Camp Hughes, Manitoba.

The smiles that anticipated a happy future faded in war. Gordon was killed in action; Dell Matheson, his girlfriend, died in the flu epidemic.

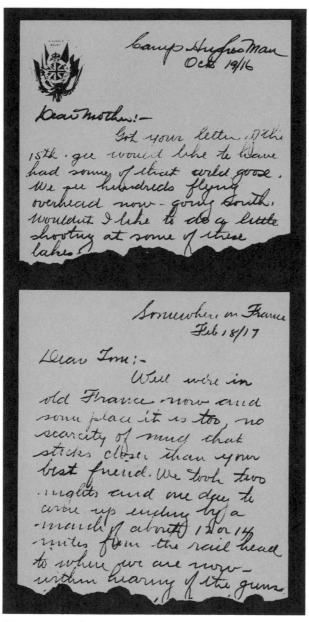

Camp Hughes Man
Oct 19/16

Dear Mother:—

Got your letter of the 15th. gee would like to have had some of that wild goose. We see hundreds flying overhead now - going south. Wouldn't I like to do a little shooting at some of these lakes.

Somewhere in France
Feb 18/17

Dear Tom:—

Well we're in old France now and some place it is too, no scarcity of mud that sticks closer than your best friend. We took two nights and one day to come up ending by a march of about 1 or 1½ miles from the rail head to where we are now — within hearing of the guns.

These excerpts from two letters home tell only part of the young private's story. Thousands of young men like Gordon Gibson endured first the homesickness of training camp, then the mud "that sticks closer than your best friend."

Mack Sennett, Fatty Arbuckle, the Keystone Cops, Mary Pickford and Theda Bara. The Chautauqua first visited Regina in the spring of 1917.

Communications between the men in the trenches and their loved ones back home were vexingly slow and unreliable. All mail had to be delivered by ship and train and, if it survived the German U-boat blockade on the North Atlantic, a letter to or from the trenches could take anywhere from three to six weeks in transit. The macabre sorrow of hearing from a son or husband, whose death in action had already been confirmed by government telegram ("I'm feeling well, and looking forward to coming home soon . . .") was all too common.

Perhaps the hardest role of all was that played by those who stayed behind. True, they enjoyed comparative comfort and lived in safety, while their men lived somewhere between the inner and outer circles of hell. But the front-line soldier at least knew if he was alive or dead. Not so his mother and father, his wife or girlfriend, his brothers and sisters. They had somehow to carry on with their ordinary lives, going to work each day, doing the chores, eating meals and sleeping without knowing from one dawn to the next whether they were wives or widows; proud parents or grief-stricken, suddenly-old men and women with empty, no-longer-needed rooms in their houses; sweethearts who would become brides only if they met someone else who could help them to forget the way it had once been.

not coming home again

"I made it a habit to write every Sunday," a Winnipeg woman recalls. "Lots of times there wasn't much to tell him, except that the weather had been good or bad, or maybe that I'd bought a new dress, but I wrote anyway, because I wanted him to always know that somebody back home cared about him. What made it hard was that I could never be sure he was still alive when I wrote those letters."

With no radio or television, people relied entirely on their daily newspapers for information on the progress of the war. The main headline and feature story almost always dealt with developments at the front, and items of local interest—casualties, honours won, enlistments, promotions, postings overseas – were sprinkled throughout the inside pages. Extensive lists of dead, wounded and missing appeared after every major engagement involving Canadian troops, and seldom did an issue appear without at least one picture of a local boy who would not be coming home again.

the war remained remote

One thing that was not a problem was the state of the economy. Within a year of the declaration of war, partly because of enlistments, Canada was near full employment, and soon there were serious labour shortages in several parts of the country. Plants manufacturing munitions, ships and planes sprang up in cities from coast to coast, and by 1917 almost one-third of all the shells fired by the armies of the British empire were manufactured in Canada. The war also provided extra stimulus to the mining of such minerals as copper, lead and nickel from the great ore-bodies of the Canadian Shield. In "the bread-basket of the world," encouraged by the record crop of 1915, western farmers took on the task of helping to feed the war-starved nations who supported the Allies. Across the country wages rose, though not as rapidly as prices.

However real, the war remained remote for most Canadians who stayed at home – something that was being fought in foreign countries several thousand miles away. Such was uniquely not the case in Halifax. For Haligonians, the western

Halifax Explodes!

On the morning of December 6, 1917, two ships collided at The Narrows near Halifax harbour, one carrying a load of explosives. When the smoke had cleared, 2,000 people were dead, an equal number were seriously injured, scattered among the city's ruins.

Details That May Assist in Identifying Hundreds of Unclaimed Bodies Which Have Been Interred

THE following particulars obtained from the unclaimed bodies compiled by A. S. Banstead, chairman of the mortuary committee, may be of value in proving identifications of persons missing since the disaster. Those seeking friends or relatives may perhaps discover items described here that will assist them in their search. Much of the clothing described it has been necessary to destroy because of its condition, but all possible has been retained and will be shown to the parties wishing to follow the clue found here.

The most common caricature in wartime newspaper and magazine cartoons was "the hated Hun." In this version, an irate "Hun" is shocked to read that the second Canadian War Loan is over-subscribed by $80 million.

POW camps were established in Canada to house German seaman from captured U-boats. These musclemen are in Amherst, N.S.

front began at the entrance to their harbour. They saw evidence of it every day. The formation of North Atlantic convoys in Bedford Basin reminded them that German U-boats were lurking almost within sight of Barrington Street. The first Canadian contingent sailed from Quebec City, but from then on Halifax became the great embarkation point, and three out of four Canadian soldiers who went overseas boarded ship at that city's Pier 2. To house the troops awaiting departure, dozens of long, depressingly grey, wooden huts were thrown up in various parts of the city.

Soon, too, there was an ebb tide back across the Atlantic, as thousands of wounded and gassed soldiers returned. Having sailed to stirring military tunes, they came back to waiting ambulances and the dismal wards of Halifax army hospitals on Cogswell Street and sprawling over Camp Hill.

Still another reminder was provided by the German and other enemy-alien prisoners housed in the Citadel and on Melville Island in Halifax harbour. Most of these were seamen who had been unlucky enough to find themselves in Canadian ports at the outbreak of hostilities, while others were citizens of various foreign countries who attempted to pass through Halifax without satisfactory passports. One of the latter was a bearded, fiery-eyed Russian Jew named Bronstein, but who preferred to call himself Leon Trotsky. In March 1917 he was taken off a ship bound for Russia (where the Bolshevik revolution was just beginning) and confined in the Citadel, where he was a quiet and model prisoner. Three months later this strange man, who was destined to become one of the most intriguing figures of the twentieth century, and to be murdered many years later in Mexico City under circumstances that have never fully been explained, was released on the request

These Vancouver veterans, one on crutches, another with a cane, man a mock dug-out in one of the city's Victory Bond campaigns.

Victory Bond stamps put the finger on everyone to support the war effort. Another version of the stamp bore the catchy message, "We lick them at the front, you lick them at the back."

of the new Soviet government and allowed to proceed by ship to Moscow.

The presence of thousands of bored and lonely Canadian soldiers and seamen from all over the world brought temporary prosperity to Halifax, but inevitably led to friction with the local people, who saw their city changed in many undesirable ways, one of which was the influx of a swarm of prostitutes from all over Canada.

On the cold morning of December 6, 1917, the war reached Halifax with terrible violence. Shortly after eight o'clock that morning the French munitions ship *Mont Blanc,* entering harbour with a cargo of time-bomb explosives, collided with the Belgian relief vessel *Imo.* An hour later the burning *Mont Blanc* exploded. The blast levelled large sections of Halifax and killed over 1,400 people outright, with another 600 to die later of their injuries. The sound was heard over most of the province. All that was ever found of the *Mont Blanc* was a cannon, which fell behind Dartmouth, and an anchor shaft weighing two tons, which landed two miles away across the Northwest Arm. Prior to the bombing raids of World War II, no city was ever so hard hit by an explosive force, and the government relief agency established to aid the victims would not close its doors until early in 1976, more than half a century later.

The war was a major influence in bringing about many changes in the lives of Canadian women, apart from the fact that it made widows of so many of them. With the rapid growth of the munitions industry and the general shortage of manpower, there was a dramatic increase in the number of women who were employed – many at jobs that would have been considered quite inappropriate prior to 1914. In Toronto and Calgary they drove streetcars; on both coasts they filled in

The Home Front

Munitions industries expanded production with Canada's increased commitment to the war. By 1916 women became a vital part of the work force, although at the early stages factory owners used every excuse to keep them in strictly menial, low-paying jobs. However, activity on the home front did not only involve making bombs. Knitting clubs were organized across the country to make stockings for the men overseas. Bond drives were so well organized that volunteers calling from house to house kept file cards on each family's subscription. Women replaced men as streetcar drivers, bank tellers, plant inspectors, and salespersons. Those unable to work were encouraged to "do their bit" folding bandages or packing parcels for the troops. Farmers were encouraged to expand production, even though many of their hired hands were away in uniform. The war had an effect on everyone.

These white-capped women are soldering fuses at the British Munitions plant at Verdun, Quebec. The average pay was 20¢ – 35¢ an hour.

All the workers in this Winnipeg factory are men. By the peak of the war production, women had filled a large percentage of these jobs, too.

The Emmeline, Manitoba, knitting club out in full force, running up a dozen stockings. For soldiers in the mudholes, a new pair was a prized possession.

These young women (and two recruits) pitch in to make this Toronto fund-raising bazaar for war aid a financial and morale-boosting success.

Christmas Time in the Trenches

You can help brighten what might otherwise be a cheerless day

THE SOLDIERS' FIELD COMFORT LEAGUE

has assembled a Christmas Box containing articles of comfort greatly needed by our Canadian Boys and Girls, which will go direct to either the trenches or any of the training camps, or the military transports of

THE DEPARTMENT OF MILITIA AND DEFENCE

RETURN POST CARD

THE OVERSEAS CHRISTMAS BOX

A MERRY CHRISTMAS — A HAPPY NEW Y.

FROM THE CITIZENS OF CANADA

"FOR LIBERTY'S IN EVERY BLOW"

JACK CANUCK PLAYING C

Cowan's CHOCOLATE

Taylors Merry Christmas TOILET SOAP

SMOKING MIXTURE

10 CIGARETTES SAFE RETURN

MADE IN CANADA

PIPE CLEANERS

Each of the League's Christmas Boxes contains the following assortment:

40 Highest grade cigarettes.	A cake of Taylor's soap.	Writing paper and envelopes.
¼ lb. Finest smoking tobacco	A box of matches.	A soft lead pencil.
1 50c. Briar pipe.	2 bars of Cowan's chocolate.	A package of pipe cleaners.
1 package of cigarette paper.	A pair of heavy shoelaces.	A return post card.
2 Khaki Hkfs.		

The whole assortment being put in a beautifully lithographed tin container.

Though the Christmas Box represents a retail value of $3.00 (including postage) the Soldiers' Field Comfort League is enabled through the generosity of some of Canada's leading manufacturers, coupled with the co-operation of the Department of Militia and Defence, to set down right in the trenches one of the Boxes for EVERY DOLLAR subscribed. A special box is now being prepared for

THE RED CROSS NURSING SISTERS

containing articles dear to the feminine heart.

DONORS at one dollar or more are privileged to name the particular soldier who should receive one of the boxes, and a card bearing the donor's name is put into the box, thus enabling the lucky soldier recipient to know just who remembered him on Christmas Day

Please make all checks payable to

THE SOLDIERS' FIELD COMFORT LEAGUE

(Organizing Offices) Suite 610, C.P.R Building, TORONTO

AND REMEMBER—

"FOR LIBERTY'S IN EVERY BLOW"—BURNS.

The contents of this Christmas package may seem pretty meagre now, but to the men a pack of cigarettes, a cake of soap and a chocolate bar were treasures.

**Nellie McClung
"Calamity Nell"**

Prohibitionist, suffragist, and one of the first MPPs in the country, the author of several novels that made her well-known and independent – this was Nellie McClung. She piloted the move for divorce legislation ("Why are pencils equipped with erasers, if not to correct mistakes?") and birth control when such things were taboo. Because of her active involvement in women's rights, her brother once cautioned her to stop agitating and "start acting like a normal person." Married, Nellie moved her family to Edmonton in 1914, and in 1921 she was elected to the Alberta legislature, where she worked for women's property rights, mother's allowance and free medical and dental care for school children. By 1919 women had the vote in almost every province, as a result (in part) of her work.

as crew members on short-handed tug-boats and fishing vessels; in the Prairies they helped bring in the wheat crops.

As a reflection of this greater involvement outside the home, there were dramatic changes in styles of dress: skirts became far less restrictive, and gradually crept up until they reached just below the knee. The trend towards less severe and more attractive fashions was also evident in the greatly increased use of lipstick and other cosmetics. A few of the very daring women even smoked cigarettes in public, although this practice was frowned upon by the vast majority of both women and men.

sisters-in-arms

In Edmonton a team of young women, coached by a teacher named Percy Page, started a basketball dynasty which was to become perhaps the most successful sports organization in the country's history. The girls, all former students at McDougall Commercial High School, became world famous as the "Edmonton Grads" and were almost unbeatable over the next quarter of a century.

Also in Edmonton, author Emily Murphy was appointed a police magistrate in 1916.

A University Women's Club was organized in Regina, and Councils of Women were active in many Canadian cities.

In every province, suffragettes – as determined as they were capable – campaigned vigorously for their demand that the right to vote be extended to women. In Saskatchewan, England's Emmeline Pankhurst drew enthusiastic audiences; in Manitoba it was the dynamic Nellie McClung; in British Columbia, Dorothy Davis; in Ontario, Flora Denison and Margaret Gordon.

The first breakthrough came in Alberta, where women were given the franchise in municipal and

civic elections in April 1916. Within a year that province, along with Saskatchewan and Manitoba, enacted suffrage legislation for provincial voting, to be followed a few months later by British Columbia.

The main goal of the sisters-in-arms was, of course, the federal franchise. As a prelude to the general election of December 1917, Borden's Union Government granted the vote to the mothers, sisters and wives of men in the armed forces. This, however, was generally seen as a political manoeuvre to help ensure enactment of Borden's conscription bill – since these women could be counted on to support compulsory military service – and thus as a somewhat tainted victory. It turned out to be almost the final battle, however, and by the time the men overseas had defeated their enemies, the women at home had won their war. National suffrage became part of the law of the land.

Many of the suffragettes were also caught up in a second, in many ways related, campaign – this one not for something (the vote), but against something (the evils of drinking). Here Nellie McClung was particularly prominent. The well-known novelist, who could command substantial fees to address anti-booze rallies, spoke often and never failed to fire both barrels at John Barleycorn. Wherever she appeared she drew overflow crowds.

Prohibition carried the day

It was the last in a long series of temperance waves that went back almost a century, and strong forces mustered behind the crusade to stamp out demon rum, spearheaded by the Woman's Christian Temperance Union. The vast majority of Protestant churchmen used their pulpits to support it. The United Grain Growers and most other farm groups were for it. So, vehemently, was the Orange

Lodge, which saw liquor as something condoned, if not promoted, by the Roman Catholic Church. The Retail Merchants' Association extended its blessing. So did most provincial medical associations. And so on.

Drinkers were urged to sign "the pledge," a card on which the bearer solemnly promised "by the help of God, to abstain from the use of all Intoxicating Liquors . . ." A Banish-the-Bar campaign was launched in the Prairie Provinces.

Saskatchewan was the first to yield to the mounting pressure. Premier Scott closed that province's bars on July 1, 1915 – a nasty way, most tipplers felt, of celebrating Dominion Day. After a provincial plebiscite, Alberta passed similar legislation in 1916, to be shortly followed by Manitoba.

In province after province Prohibition carried the day, so that by the time "the boys" came home following the armistice of 1918, it would not be to their favourite saloons and bars.

Only in Quebec did booze survive – another of the many ways in which the province was finding itself increasingly isolated from the nation.

As the months of the war lengthened into years, bringing changes and upheavals of many kinds, and as more and more names were added to the Honour Rolls of those who had given their lives for their country, it became clear that the men of the Canadian Expeditionary Force, courageous from the beginning, had become as competent in battle as any troops serving on the western front. A country with almost no military tradition had produced an army of the very first rank.

Those who were left behind to live with the agonies of uncertainty or the sadness of bereavement could take pride in that. And in the knowledge that they were doing their best to support their loved ones who had gone overseas.

Among the popular war songs like "Pack Up Your Troubles In Your Old Kit Bag" and "It's A Long Way To Tipperary," it was appropriate that at least one looked *westward* across the Atlantic for its focus.

A beautiful, poignant melody, more a hymn than a ballad, it was called "Keep The Home Fires Burning."

Three of the world's most outspoken campaigners for women's rights are front and centre in this rare photo taken on the steps of the McClung house in Edmonton; British suffrage leader Emmeline Pankhurst is flanked by Emily Murphy (right) and Nellie "Calamity Nell" McClung (left).

"Over There"

Sheet music printed during the war years used a stunning array of patriotic colours and catchy titles, and any home with a piano usually had a stack of them piled on the Heintzman. Most town and city parks still had a band-shell, and on Sunday afternoons people would gather there to listen to the local band (usually made up of men over the military age) launch into a rousing march. There was a clear purpose to most of these songs–to keep the spirits up. And even at the bleakest moments in the war, you could probably hear someone whistling "Over There."

This flag, bearing the inscription "Take it, wave it, and bring it back," led the St. Catharines, Ontario militia overseas. The signatures written across the ensign are the names of the soldiers who fought, and some who died, under the banner. The bullet holes and powder burns that decorate the flag tell the story of this unit's battles.

CHAPTER SEVEN

"D'Ye Ken Sam Hughes?"

You cannot understand how sick we all were of the war, nor our anxiety of finishing it as soon as possible, if there was any chance of success.

Sir Arthur Currie, 1919.

"Over there" the military decisions that would provide the fodder for future historians – and more immediately meant life or death for millions of ordinary soldiers – were made by a relative handful of men in the high commands of the opposing armies.

However individually different the generals and field marshals might have been in other respects, as career officers they tended to share certain in-bred, basic characteristics. Their profession had trained them to regard casualties as a way of keeping score; the success of an attack, a battle, or a whole campaign could be dispassionately evaluated by comparing actual losses suffered in the field with estimates worked out beforehand.

Knowing that their security and their hopes for advancement depended upon achieving results in the field, they were inclined to grow restless and throw their troops into ill-conceived engagements, in the belief that any action, however empty of expectations, was better than no action. Prolonged inactivity would not provide a fertile ground for promotions. This impatience, often coupled with incompetence, exacted a terrible toll.

They were conservative men, schooled in the military traditions of the nineteenth century and slow to adapt to changed circumstances. Once the struggle settled down into trench warfare, neither side had the striking power to break out of the deadly impasse – the new tanks that appeared in 1916 and 1917 were primitive and unreliable, more important psychologically than practically; and air support continued to be limited to reconnaissance and artillery-spotting. The tactics of *blitzkrieg* would have to await another world war.

Meanwhile the generals of the western front showed little inclination or ability to innovate. To a terrible extent their "know-how" consisted of sending wave after wave of men into murderous assaults upon insignificant and unattainable objectives. The fact that hundreds of thousands of infantrymen unhesitatingly obeyed these orders was both tribute to their devotion and courage, and testimony to the extent of their tragedy.

Of all the inadequate military tacticians none came under heavier fire than Field Marshal Sir Douglas Haig, Supreme Commander of the British Forces (including the Canadian Corps). British Prime Minister Lloyd George would later characterize Haig's overall "strategy" as no more than "a bovine and brutal game of attrition," and attribute his incompetence to a "narrow and stubborn egotism, unsurpassed among the records of disaster."

Each wartime package of Cowan's Cocoa contained one of these collector's cards. Major-general was the second highest rank among Canadian officers.

Arthur Currie
Commander of the Canadian Corps

Canada's greatest soldier and strategist of WWI, Arthur William Currie began his career in the army as just "an amateur Saturday-night soldier." He was born on a farm in Middlesex Co., Ont., in 1875 and studied to be a schoolteacher. At the age of eighteen, he went to British Columbia, sold insurance and real estate, and rose in the militia to the rank of lieutenant-colonel. In Aug. 1914 he was dispatched overseas. His tactical command at Ypres, St. Julien and Vimy Ridge earned him the rank of major-general and the leadership of the Canadian Corps. On Nov. 10, 1918, hours before the cease-fire, his troops recaptured the Belgian town of Mons. The action was sharply criticized in Parliament by Currie's arch-rival, Sir Sam Hughes, as an act of personal glory-seeking. Currie worked ten years to clear himself on the charge. He retired from the military in 1920, and was named principal and vice-chancellor of McGill, a post he held until death.

Among those who clashed with Haig was Brigadier-General Arthur Currie, who took over command of the Canadian Corps in June 1917. Intelligent, able, tough, Brigadier-General Currie was fiercely proud of his soldiers, and steadfast in his determination to safeguard their battle-won rights. He refused to serve under the British General Gough, whom he considered to be grossly inadequate. He reluctantly agreed to commit his command to Haig's brutal Passchendaele offensive only after being assured that the Canadian divisions would fight together as a force, and only on condition that he himself approve the date of their commitment to the battle.

Currie was one of the designers of the great push at Amiens in August 1918, and later that year his brilliant plan to avoid the suicidal frontal attack on the Canal du Nord originally conceived by the British high command undoubtedly saved a great many Canadian lives. Currie, a former real estate agent on the west coast, was one of the most able generals of the war, and he enjoyed the respect of his men because they knew that he would stand behind them.

a collective affair

At home Borden, too, was fighting for a greater Canadian share in determining the policies of the empire. Prior to 1914 it had been tacitly accepted that foreign policy for the British Empire would be manufactured in London and exported to the dominions and colonies. The far-flung chickens would then automatically respond to the clucking of the mother hen. But, in view of Canada's massive contribution to the war, Borden was no longer satisfied with that arrangement. In January 1916 he wrote to a colleague:

It can hardly be expected that we shall put 400,000 or 500,000 men in the field, and willingly accept the position of having no more voice, and receiving no more consideration, than if we were toy automata. Any person cherishing such an expectation harbours an unfortunate and even dangerous delusion.

In 1917, largely through his insistence, an Imperial War Cabinet was established, which included the prime ministers of the self-governing dominions. From then on the conduct of the war became much more a collective affair, worked out through continuous consultation between London and the satellite capitals of the Empire.

a peculiar temperament

From before the outbreak of war until late in 1916 Borden had to contend with one of the most bizarre and astonishing personalities in all of Canadian history – his Minister of Militia, Sam Hughes, later to become Sir Sam Hughes.

While no one questioned Hughes' dedication, there was equally no doubt as to his arrogance, his thick-skinned rudeness, or his paranoid conviction that he was surrounded by enemies, jealous incompetents and fools determined to frustrate his every turn.

"There is only one feeling as to Sam," Sir George Foster, Minister of Trade and Commerce wrote; "that he is crazy."

A decade later, when Borden wrote his memoirs, he had this to say about Hughes:

While he was a man of marked ability . . . his temperament was so peculiar, and his actions and language so unusual . . . that one was inclined to doubt his usefulness as a Minister . . . . He was under constant illusions that enemies were working against him . . . and [often] his conduct and speech were so eccentric as to justify the conclusion that his mind was unbalanced.

Nevertheless, employing a combination of outright bullying and occasional deceit, the minister of militia managed to have his way with the temperamentally gentle Borden much of the time. Hughes was capable of gloating over this. "Mr. Borden is a most lovely fellow," he confided to a friend, "gentle-hearted as a girl."

During the first two years of the war Colonel Sam was involved in any number of controversial issues. As an Orangeman, he imposed a highly unpopular ban on wet canteens in all militia camps, and habitually went out of his way to show his distaste for everything Roman Catholic and French.

He was the die-hard champion of the infamous Ross rifle long after almost all field commanders had denounced it as hopeless. When one of his female secretaries invented the McAdam shovel– a spade with a hole in the middle, to be used as a combined trenching tool and bullet-proof shield for snipers – Hughes ordered thousands of them. They shortly proved to be utterly useless in the field, and were sold as scrap for a minute fraction of their original cost.

Hughes was also largely responsible for the fact that the first Canadian soldiers to go into the lines were issued with boots that quickly rotted and disintegrated in the dampness and mud.

contracts and corruption

Typically, Colonel Sam assumed autocratic control over the purchase of munitions and armaments, appointing men whose personal allegiance he could trust, many of whom he had made honorary colonels, as buying agents. Several of these worked on behalf of the Shell Committee, which Hughes created in 1915. One, a freelance commission-man named J. Wesley Allison, negotiated several million dollars worth of contracts, principally in the United States. By the summer of

Returning from the front in muddy uniform, boots that are probably falling apart, smoking his last cigarette, the only things on the mind of this Canadian "Tommy" are a bath and some dry clothes

The Arsenal of War

Gunners and drivers of the Motor Machine Gun Detachment clean up their steel-clad vehicles after muddy, bloody battles at the Somme in France.

Col. Sam Hughes oversees a demonstration of the Ross rifle and McAdam shovel. In combat both of these Hughes-approved items were next to useless.

This photo shows one of the oldest as well as one of the newest elements in the arsenal. WW I was the last war for horses and the first for poison gas.

Again, the oldest and the most revolutionary machines of war: horse-drawn ammunition caissons pass motor trucks. Note the observation balloon.

Heavy howitzers and artillery went under a dozen different nicknames like "Kill Joy." It took five or six men just to load and fire the gun shown above.

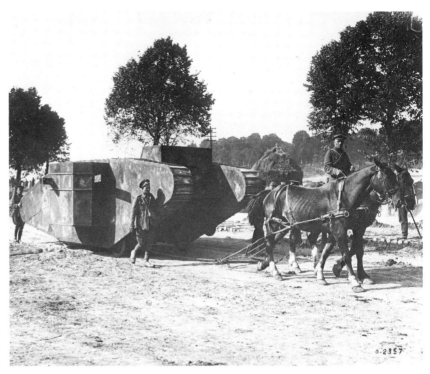

Tanks that looked like this were first used in combat in 1917 by the Allies. This one, however, is a plywood dummy put together to deceive the enemy.

Another of the curiosities of WW I – the carrier pigeon. Years before wireless walkie-talkies, birds were trained to carry coded messages along the front.

A soldier is busy chalking a few hasty messages onto these 15 inch shells. One of these shells could tear a good sized hole in a city block.

The Crisis at Home

HOW LAURIER "LEADS" QUEBEC

L'ARMEE ANGLAISE

LES BLOATED COLONIALS

QUEBEC BOLSHEVIK

DOING HIS BIT IN THE GREAT WAR

HE'LL WANT TO KNOW

"Daddy, how did you vote in the Big War Election?"

There's nothing subtle in these cartoons from Canadian newspapers of Dec. 1917. The French are drawn as anarchists and quitters, English Canadians (top-right) as lackeys of John Bull.

1916 there were many charges, both in the press and in the House of Commons, that some of Hughes' appointees were growing rich through influence-peddling, kick-backs and other forms of corruption.

At about the same time the decision was finally taken to replace the Ross rifle, for so long stubbornly defended by Hughes, with the British Lee-Enfield.

Colonel Sam's flamboyant but erratic star was rapidly waning. Borden appointed a Royal Commission to look into "irregularities" in the purchasing of arms and munitions, and while its subsequent findings were inconclusive – except in the case of Allison, who was proven to have accepted kick-backs – the mere launching of the inquiry constituted a severe reprimand to Hughes.

The minister of militia continued to act independently, often ignoring Borden's instructions and more than once flagrantly defying the prime minister. He seemed determined to run his department, Borden noted, "as if it were a distinct and separate government in itself." At long last coming to the conclusion that Hughes "cannot remain in the government," Borden asked for his resignation. It was forthcoming on November 11, 1916 – two years to the day before the Armistice would be signed.

recruiting dropped off

By early 1917 the Canadian Corps was facing a serious shortage of manpower. Battle losses had been grievous, and recruiting had dropped off steadily through 1916. Even using the Fifth Division for reinforcements, it was becoming increasingly difficult to keep the four divisions already committed to the front up to strength.

In the spring of that year Borden returned from an Imperial Conference in London, convinced that compulsory military service, something he had consistently rejected until then, could no longer be avoided.

"It is apparent to me that the voluntary system will not yield further substantial results," he told Parliament. "It is my duty to announce to the House that early proposals will be made to provide, by compulsory military enlistment on a selective basics, such reinforcements as may be necessary to maintain the Canadian Army in the field."

voices against conscription

The announcement touched off an emotional earthquake that was to shake the country from coast to coast, and lay bare faults and fissures in the federal crust created by Confederation.

A great many individuals, and most farm groups and labour organizations, were staunchly against "conscription." But the most consolidated and outspoken opposition came from the province of Quebec.

The legacy left by Sam Hughes had an important influence in this. The former minister of militia had gone out of his way to taunt and anger the Roman Catholics in Quebec. In spite of the noble combat record of the famed "Vandoos" (the Royal Twenty-Second Regiment of Quebec), no attempt had been made to place French Canadian volunteers in French-speaking units: Colonel Sam seemed to think it was good for them to have to learn to take orders in English. And many of the recruiting agents in Quebec were Protestant ministers.

Still more provocative was legislation enacted in Ontario and Manitoba to restrict or eliminate the teaching of the French language in provincial schools. Why, many French Canadians asked, should we die for an empire and a country that denies us our historic and constitutional rights?

A legion of Quebec voices spoke out against conscription from pulpits, platforms and rostrums, but two were paramount: they belonged to two familiar, but very different, antagonists of Borden – Sir Wilfrid Laurier and Henri Bourassa.

Laurier, growing old but still firm in his convictions, had consistently been moderate, temperate and co-operative in his attitudes toward the war. From the beginning he had supported the Conservative government, agreeing to extend the life of Parliament by a year in the conviction that circumstances required a temporary end to partisan politics. He had urged the youth of his native province to enlist, pleading from conviction that the issues involved justified personal sacrifice. But he had pledged to do his best to see that no man would be sent overseas against his will. And he did not view compulsory service as a practical solution.

"How many men will conscription bring in?" he asked. "Just a few slackers, exactly the same as in England . . ."

Above all, Laurier was concerned that the issue should not be allowed to tear asunder the social and political fabric of the nation, to which he had dedicated the whole of his long career. Extremist positions and posturings must be avoided at all costs.

political oratory and patriotic phrases

Bourassa was far less restrained, far more intemperate. If he did not actively urge rebellion in the editorial pages of *Le Devoir,* he acknowledged it to be an almost inevitable result. And his chief lieutenant, Armand Lavergne, advocated disobedience to the Compulsory Service Bill. *"Vive la liberté!"* he exhorted a huge audience in Montreal. *"Vive l'indépendance!"*

Opposition to conscription was by no means limited to Quebec, but it found its most organized and cohesive expression in that province. In other parts of the country patriotic and jingoistic senti-

Slander!
That man is a slanderer who says that
The Farmers of Ontario
will vote with
Bourassa, Pro-Germans,
Suppressors of Free Speech and Slackers
Never!
They Will Support Union Government
Citizens' Union Committee

In 1917 the war became a home front issue, and the election campaign of December became one of propaganda posters. Conscription was the question every voter had to consider before he or she marked the ballot. Political feelings in Quebec, championed by Henri Bourassa, Armand Lavergne and others were solidly against drafting Canadians to die in the European war. This ad from The Farmer's Advocate *leaves no doubt about the stance taken by the farmers of Ontario on the question.*

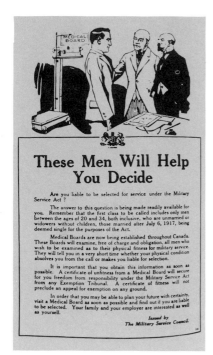

These Men Will Help You Decide

Are you liable to be selected for service under the Military Service Act?

The answer to this question is being made readily available for you. Remember that the first class to be called includes only men between the ages of 20 and 34, both inclusive, who are unmarried or widowers without children, those married after July 6, 1917, being deemed single for the purposes of the Act.

Medical Boards are now being established throughout Canada. These Boards will examine, free of charge and obligation, all men who wish to be examined as to their physical fitness for military service. They will tell you in a very short time whether your physical condition absolves you from the call or makes you liable for selection.

It is important that you obtain this information as soon as possible. A certificate of unfitness from a Medical Board will secure for you freedom from responsibility under the Military Service Act from any Exemption Tribunal. A certificate of fitness will not preclude an appeal for exemption on any ground.

In order that you may be able to plan your future with certainty, visit a Medical Board as soon as possible and find out if you are liable to be selected. Your family and your employer are interested as well as yourself.

Issued by
The Military Service Council.

In 1917, for the first time in history Canadian men eligible for military service were required by an act of Parliament to serve in the army. Men between the ages of 20 and 34 who were single were the first to report to the local medical board for a fitness test.

ments in favour of Borden's proposed legislation were also hardening.

Outside of Quebec Laurier's support fell away day by day. Sir Clifford Sifton, the most influential of all western Liberals, defected again to back Borden; so did many other former supporters of Sir Wilfrid in Ontario and the Maritimes.

Borden decided to consolidate his position by creating a "Union Government," in which ten pro-conscription Liberals accepted posts as cabinet ministers and parliamentary assistants. Still, the prime minister felt compelled to "go to the country" on the issue of compulsory service.

The resulting election campaign of 1917 was a bitter one, steeped with passions and emotions. In Quebec there was much inflammatory talk of defiance, and some discussion of possible secession from Confederation; elsewhere the political oratory rang with patriotic phrases, and was often flagrantly anti-Catholic, anti-French and anti-Quebec.

Borden used every means open to him to ensure the result he wanted, the result he was convinced the nation must deliver if Canada were to pursue its war effort successfully. Mothers, wives and sisters of men in the armed forces, who could be expected to endorse conscription, were given the

vote by act of Parliament; immigrants from Germany, Austria and other enemy countries who had been in Canada for less than fifteen years, and might oppose it, were summarily disenfranchised. And many claimed that the soldier vote, solidly pro-conscription, was distributed so as to do the government the most good, regardless of the constituencies from which the enlisted men came.

On the evening of election day the results spread slowly westward as the polls closed in each time zone. The trend was evident by the time Ontario had been heard from, Borden and his Union Government sweeping eight of the nine provinces in a great show of strength.

What the summing up revealed, however, was not a nation united but a nation terribly, perhaps mortally, divided. In Quebec, solidly against the rest of the country, Laurier's anti-conscription Liberals had taken all but three of the sixty-five seats.

The French Canadian province stood alone, isolated and beleaguered.

The Union Government had gained its mandate, but in the process the wedge had been cruelly driven deeper between the nation's two founding heritages, the French and the English.

New names in Canadian history. More are coming — Will you be there?

ENLIST!

Make us as proud of you as we are of him!

LOOK ON This Picture and On That!

THE FATE OF THE EMPIRE DEPENDS ON **YOU!**
COME WITH US IN THE
215TH

And help defend it. There's a place waiting. It is your DUTY to fight for those you love

Lieut.-Col. HARRY COCKSHUTT, Officer Commanding, 215th Overseas Battalion, C.E.F.

EVERYWOMAN'S WORLD
Canada's Magazine for Canada's Women

CONTAINS THE LAST WORD IN FALL FASHIONS

The Amiable Pretenders, By Eleanor Hoyt Brainerd, Complete In This Issue

SEPTEMBER 1918 · Continental Publishing Company, Limited, Toronto, Canada · TWENTY CENTS

Nº 231896

Everywoman's World, *the most popular and outspoken magazine of women's opinion in the era, championed the fight for voting rights, equal pay and property ownership.*

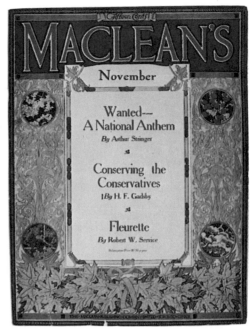

MACLEAN'S
November

Wanted—
A National Anthem
By Arthur Stringer

Conserving the
Conservatives
By H. F. Gadsby

Fleurette
By Robert W. Service

A string of top writers filled the pages of John Bayne Maclean's national magazine.

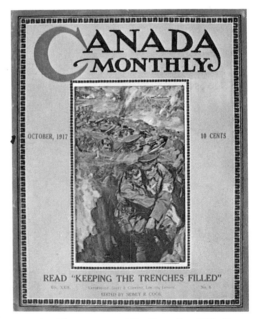

CANADA MONTHLY

OCTOBER, 1917 · 10 CENTS

READ "KEEPING THE TRENCHES FILLED"

Articles like "Keeping The Trenches Filled" were regular war features in Canada Monthly.

Poster War

Recruiting posters, bond drive posters, fund raising posters. . . WW I was a poster war. Tacked on the walls of banks, post offices, churches, and other public buildings, these graphic reminders used the best devices of advertising to get their points across. The war effort depended on two resources: money and men, and even if the message was sometimes too strong or the appeal too dramatic, most Canadians met their obligation to help when called upon. "If you cannot join him, you should help her" was a common slogan used to raise money for the Patriotic Fund for servicemen's wives, orphans and widows. "Essex men are not cowards" worked to fill the ranks of a rural Ontario militia unit, and communities throughout the country witnessed a similar response. Despite strong ties to the Empire in English-speaking Canada, many posters played down loyalties to the "mother country." Posters in Quebec translated the war into a struggle to preserve the democratic foundations of Europe. After all, France, not England, was being over-run by the "dreadful Hun." How did Canada react to the poster war? Over 400,000 troops served overseas; well over $1 *billion* was spent by private and commercial investors on war bonds; and over $47 million was turned over to the Canadian Patriotic Fund. Call them what you will, propaganda or "hard-sell" ads, posters certainly got the message across.

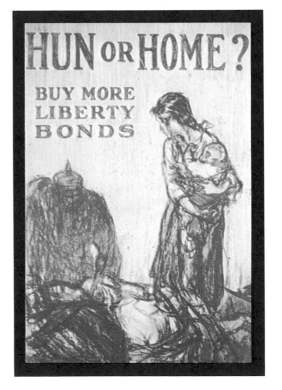

J.D. CARRICK
·60·

CHAPTER EIGHT

Aces Wild!

The aeroplane is an invention of the devil and will never play any part in such a serious business as the defence of a nation, my boy!

Colonel Sam Hughes to J.A.D. McCurdy, 1914.

When war broke out the history of the airplane, inaugurated by the Wright brothers in 1903, spanned a mere eleven years.

Most European nations had a few military planes, but generals and admirals were uniformly sceptical of their usefulness in combat, at most conceding that they might be employed for scouting over enemy lines.

Their lack of enthusiasm is easily understood. The aircraft of the day were cumbersome, flimsy affairs, held together by baling wire. Every flight was an adventure, almost as apt to end in a crash as in a safe landing. Engines could crank up no more than 100 horsepower and maximum speeds ranged from 60 to 80 miles an hour – which was about as long as they could stay in the air without landing to refuel. None was equipped with armament of any kind.

Canada had no air force of its own, requests for a small appropriation to start one having been turned down in 1910 and again in 1912. Nevertheless, close to twenty-five thousand Canadians became involved in the war in the skies by joining the British Royal Flying Corps, and were among the best airmen to fight on either side.

Since the development of the airplane was so recent, there was no history of aerial combat. In this area at least, the young Canadians did not suffer from lack of experience and tradition. They seemed somehow to have been born to the cockpit, as if duelling in the air came naturally to them. As the war progressed, Canada could boast of having more than her share of flying "aces."

During the first few months of hostilities pilots of the opposing armies flew their faltering Blériots, Farmans and Rumplers on reconnaissance missions over enemy lines with neither the inclination nor the equipment to attack one another. Before long, however, they began to devise ways of locking horns in the sky. Some carried rifles, pistols, shotguns. Others threw bricks or lengths of rusty chain in an attempt to foul opposing propellers. A few dangled lead weights on long wires for the same purpose.

In time pilots began experimenting with machine guns. At first they were of very limited value because they had to be mounted in a fixed position so that they fired over or around the propeller. Thus the pilot had great difficulty in attaining accuracy, and he was limited to one belt of cartridges since it was impossible to reload in the air.

What was needed was a weapon that could be controlled directly from the cockpit – which meant that it had to be able to fire *through* the propeller-

Young Men Rule the Air

WITHOUT our valorous young aviators our gunners and our troops would work in the dark.

High above the lines these daring aerial warriors are in constant communication with the commanders on the ground, guarding our troops and exposing the secrets of the Hun.

Greater scope for individual bravery and initiative could hardly be imagined.

There are opportunities for young men to achieve greatness very rapidly in the Air Service. A clear brain, a sound physique, a keenness for achievement, a fair education—are the essential qualifications.

Young men accepted as cadets receive $1.10 per day during their period of training for commissions as flying officers.

Class 1 men under the M.S. Act are eligible for the Air Service. Men 18 to 50 years of age who wish to enroll as cadets should apply personally or in writing to one of the following addresses.

Imperial **Royal Flying Corps**

Officially Canada had no air force until 1918, but young flyers, mostly from the West, won their wings in the RFC.

Opposite page: *Almost everyone has heard of the legendary "Red Baron," the greatest German flyer of WW I. But very few know that it was Capt. Roy Brown (rear), a rookie from Carleton Place, Ont., who shot down the Baron (centre) in April, 1918.*

Relaxing the Tension with a good Gillette Shave

A day a-wing over enemy lines scouting, observing, fighting, dodging shells and machine-gun bullets—is a nervous strain that has no precedent and probably no equal. When our airmen alight at last, after flights an eagle might envy, they certainly do enjoy the refreshing relaxation of a cool, smooth Gillette shave.

Nor is this appreciation of the Gillette Safety Razor limited to our airmen, or even to our own British armies. Every service has its own tense moments, hours or days, with its welcome intervals of relaxation when the Gillette is a friend indeed. Keen, compact, always ready for action, the Gillette Safety Razor is treasured in tens of thousands of kits on every fighting line on land and sea—and by no means least in the land of its birth, with the forces of our newest Ally.

Nor does its service end here, for "the man behind the man behind the gun", who in the factory, the office or on the land is bending every energy towards production —he too gets solid comfort and satisfaction out of the Gillette Safety Razor and its wonderful three minute shave.

Spend a five dollar bill to get a Gillette for one of your defenders—and get one for yourself to see how much he'll appreciate it.

The safety razor was a new gadget on the market, and a relief to men who had for years endured the nicks of the well-stropped straight razor. This ad features a lucky RAF airman enjoying the thrill of his first Gillette shave. The razor cost $5.

Before the war, Canada had only one reputable flying school. By 1918 thousands of cadets had been trained as pilots or observers. These cadets at the School of Military Aeronautics are getting a few pointers on the JN-4, the standard trainer in 1917.

thrust. By late 1915 this seemingly insurmountable problem had been solved – first through the inventiveness of men like Eugène Gilbert and Roland Garros, who inserted V-shaped wedges of metal plate into the propeller to deflect the small proportion of bullets that struck it; later by the development of more sophisticated mechanisms which synchronized the rate of firing with the revolutions-per-minute, so that there no longer was any danger of shooting off your own propeller.

When this evolution was completed, the first true fighter planes took to the skies over the western front and the era of flying aces was at hand. The word "ace" was a popular sobriquet of the time, being used particularly to describe sports heroes. The first pilot to earn the title was probably Roland Garros, who used his new through-the-propeller machine gun to shoot down five German planes in two weeks early in 1915, and was awarded the Legion of Honour.

Soon every country on both sides would have its share of legendary airmen, their names becoming household words, and their recorded "kills" being followed like the goal-scoring prowess of great hockey players in another era.

The war these young men fought had almost nothing in common with the life of filth and mud and shell shock endured by the infantrymen over whose trenches they flew. Pilots of all nations were members of an elite and very exclusive club. They lived in comparatively comfortable quarters, were attended by personal batmen, ate well, drank freely of good wines and liquors.

Flying their precarious, balky, still primitive Nieuports, Fokkers, Sopwith Camels and Spads, they were doing something that no one had ever

Major Ray Collishaw (6th from left) and a group of airmen in France in July 1918, standing in front of their brand new aircraft. Airplane design and technology made great advances during the war years, improving air speed, handling and reliability.

done before. They made the rules and developed the techniques as they went along.

There was a strong sense of camaraderie among them, foe as well as friend, and a peculiar chivalry like that once shared by feudal knights. A German *oberleutenant*, shot down behind the Allied lines, was taken to a nearby RFC airdrome, where he was royally entertained in the officers' mess and toasted with flowing champagne. The following morning the Canadian pilot whose machine gun bursts had brought the *oberleutenant* crashing down flew a solo mission over the German base, and dropped a message announcing that the captured flier was unhurt and in good spirits.

Because the risk of death was very great and ever-present, they were profoundly fatalistic. A favourite airmen's ballad, sung to the tune of "The Lost Chord," had these words:

We meet neath the sounding rafters,
The walls around us are bare;
They echo the peals of laughter –
It seems that the dead are there.
So, stand by your glasses steady,
This is a world of lies.
Here's a toast to the dead already;
Hurrah for the next man who dies.

From similar necessity, they also developed a ribald, grizzly sense of humour:

Oh, the bold aviator was dying,
And, as 'neath the wreckage he lay,
To the sobbing mechanics about him,
These last parting words did he say:

Two valves you'll find in my stomach,
Three sparkplugs are safe in my lung,
The prop is in splinters inside me,

Ray Collishaw
The Kid from Nanaimo

A born leader with a deadly aim, Raymond Collishaw was second only to Billy Bishop in the list of top Commonwealth aces of WWI. He came from Nanaimo, B.C., and after Naval College joined the naval protection service in 1908 when he was 15. Just after the war began he enrolled in the air force and during the next three years shot down 60 German aircraft. He served with the Royal Air Force in Russia and the Middle East after the war and fought in Africa during the Second World War as Air Commodore. He was promoted to acting air vice-marshal in 1942 and retired the next year after an amazing flying career of 28 years.

**Billy Bishop
Canada's Top Fighter Ace**

On the morning of June 2, 1917, in the vicinity of Cambrai, France, a twenty-three year old rookie pilot named Billy Bishop shot down three enemy aircraft, becoming the first Canadian to win the Victoria Cross. He was born in Owen Sound, Ontario, in 1894, when flying machines were pure science fiction. A born hell-raiser, he chafed under the discipline of Kingston's Royal Military College, then surprised his superiors by blossoming into a superb aerial killer when sent to France in 1915. From his open-cockpit, single-engine plane, he gunned down 72 enemy aircraft in combat before the war was over, a record that placed him among the top three fighter aces of the world. In 1919 along with another Canadian ace, Billy Barker, he founded one of the first commerical aviation companies in the country. He was the author of three books, among them the action-packed account of his battles, *Winged Warfare* (1919).

To my fingers the joy-stick is clung.

And get you six brandies and sodas,
And lay them all out in a row,
And get you six other good airmen,
To drink this pilot below.

Take the cylinders out of my kidneys,
The connecting rod out of my brain,
From the small of my back take the crankshaft,
And assemble the engine again.

Yet, unlike the foot-soldiers in the trenches, their time of exposure to death was limited to a highly acute hour or two a day. And, again unlike the infantrymen, for whom survival was to a considerable extent a matter of luck, determined by the chance pattern of indiscriminate shelling or the sweep of an enemy machine gun, combat in the air typically took the form of a personal one-on-one duel. Immediate, intimate, where you could see the face of the enemy and remember the expression. To a considerable extent an athletic contest, where fast reactions counted, and the outcome depended upon skill and experience more than the roll of distant dice. Not that luck wasn't a good thing to have on your side.

Roy Brown and the Red Baron

Germany had several aces, including Ernst Udet, Max Immelmann and others, but the most famous by far was a Prussian nobleman, Baron Manfred von Richthofen, remembered variously as the "Red Baron" or "Red Knight." Richthofen, a cold, haughty aristocrat, flew a bright crimson Fokker triplane at the head of his notorious "Flying Circus," and was credited with a total of eighty victories – the most recorded by any flier on either side.

The Red Baron finally met his end on April 21, 1918, being shot down and crashing to his death near the Bray-Corbie road behind the British lines.

Moments before he plunged to earth, Richthofen was on the tail of a young Canadian pilot, Lieutenant Wilfred "Wop" May. Behind the German ace, in turn, was another Canadian pilot, Captain Roy Brown, flying a Sopwith Camel. Brown fired several bursts, then watched Richthofen fall away in a deadly spin. It was later claimed that the fatal bullets were fired by an Australian anti-aircraft unit on the ground, but the consensus of opinion is that it was Captain Roy Brown who wrote *finis* to the blazing career of the leader of the Flying Circus.

dog-fights in the sky

The British thrilled to the exploits of a curly-haired, devil-may-care young aviator from Nottingham, Captain Albert Ball. A true maverick, with little regard for either discipline or personal safety, Ball was awarded the Victoria Cross posthumously after being shot out of the sky on May 7, 1917. He was just twenty-one years old when he died.

The French boasted flyers like the great Georges Guynemer, and the brilliant René Fonck. After the U.S. came into the war in 1917, the names of American airmen like Captain Eddie Rickenbacker, Lieutenant Frank Luke, and Major Raoul Lufbery soon rose to prominence.

In view of its small population, however, no country had more top-ranked fighting pilots than Canada. Of the twenty-seven British aces credited with thirty or more aerial victories by war's end, ten were Canadians and they included two out of the top five scorers in the whole war.

In the spring of 1917 a five-plane flight of jet-black Sopwith triplanes, headed by Nanaimo's Ray Collishaw, became the scourge of the skies over the western front. Collishaw's wingmen were Ellis Reid of Toronto, J.E. Sharman of Winnipeg, J.E. Nash of Hamilton, and Mark Alexander of

Montreal. None of the pilots was over twenty years of age. Their planes were christened *Black Roger, Black Sheep, Black Maria, Black Prince* and *Black Death.*

Day after day Collishaw and his cohorts increased their score of Albatros D-3's, Aviatiks, Halberstadts and Fokkers. They took on Richthofen's Circus in one of the great dog-fights of the war and came away clear winners. In June and July, 1917, they cleared the skies of an amazing eighty-seven German aircraft. Before hostilities came to an end Collishaw had extended his personal total to sixty confirmed kills and been awarded the DSO, the DSC and the Croix de Guerre.

little use for caution

W.A. "Billy" Bishop was an often reckless, apparently quite fearless pilot who didn't care whether he took on a lone enemy or flew into the middle of half the German airforce. Bishop was by nature a loner, spending long hours in the air on solitary hunts, and he liked to bring his Nieuport single-seater diving down on an unsuspecting victim from great heights. He was a superb marksman, a skill he had first developed as a boy by shooting squirrels with a .22 rifle in the woods near his Owen Sound home. Far from being a smooth, natural pilot, he regarded any landing he could walk away from as a good one. But when he smelled combat and swung to meet it, with the wind whistling through the struts and wires of his Nieuport, there was none better on the western front. By war's end he had been awarded the Victoria Cross (for singlehandedly destroying an enemy airdrome), and registered seventy-two victories – third best among *all* World War I flyers.

Like Bishop, Major William George Barker of Dauphin, Manitoba, seemed to find a natural joy in combat, and he, too, had little use for caution in the air. For him the more enemy aircraft there

A Comic View of the R.A.F.

Cartoonist air cadet Hendry pokes fun at the shenanigans in the RAF training school at Camp Borden, Ont. The first trainers were plywood and canvas strung together with wire, and accidents were quite common. The spectre of black clouds was often enough to keep neophytes indoors.

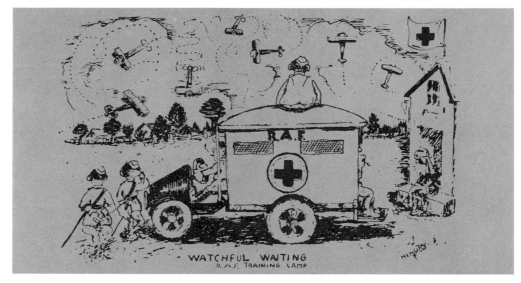

97

Canada's Flying Aces

Airplanes were still a novelty in 1914, only a few Canadian pilots were trained beyond the basics, and there were virtually no airfields. But despite these handicaps ten Canadians earned their stripes among the 27 aces of the RAF. To qualify for the distinction a flyer had to have five victories–and that meant knocking down the enemy by any means available, grenades, hand guns or rifles. With the invention of the synchronized machine gun capable of shooting through the propeller, the cat-and-mouse game of fighter pilots became a daring, deadly business.

Fitness requirements for cadet airmen were detailed and strict. Those who qualified carried their cards with pride.

Billy Barker, a 23-year-old pilot from Dauphin, Man., took on three enemy squadrons (60 planes) over Cambrai, France, and shot down six of them before he crash-landed. Total victories – 50.

Roy Brown, the man who shot down Baron Manfred von Richthofen (see page 92). The "Red Baron" was his 12th kill.

Captain Arthur Whealy, a crackshot with 19 victories to his credit, watches two mechanics affixing bombs to his Sopwith Camel. By the last phases of the war, tactics had changed from man-to-man to group operations. The belted leather jacket, helmet and goggles and breeches remained standard RAF issue.

This "bread basket" is the gondola of a balloon used for aerial reconnaissance, and the square box on the tripod is a late model moving picture camera, ready for ascent with the kinematographer.

were in the sky, the greater the opportunity to add to his score. On October 27, 1918 – just two weeks before the signing of the Armistice – Barker took off from behind the western front to fly to England, where he was to become an instructor of new pilots. He had long since established his credentials as an ace, and this was to be a routine flight into comfortable, well-earned retirement.

But, as he flew parallel to the battle front, Barker spotted a German two-seater patrolling behind the lines. Reacting instinctively, he turned to the attack. Within seconds he found himself and his new Sopwith Snipe engaged in a David-and-Goliath struggle with at least fifty German aircraft. The air was crisscrossed with tracer bullets and Barker's plane was riddled. The Canadian zoomed, darted and dove all over the sky. He shot down a German triplane . . . another . . . a Fokker D-7. But he was wounded again and again. A Spandau slug slammed into his right thigh. Another pierced the muscles of his other leg. A third shattered an elbow. Bleeding from his several wounds, slipping in and out of consciousness, Barker not only managed to keep the crippled Snipe in the air, but continued to press the attack. It was one of the most magnificent one-man-shows of the entire war. His fuel tank was punctured, but he was able to switch to a reserve supply.

time and luck

Inevitably time and luck ran out for Barker and his shot-up aircraft. Breaking off the engagement, he glided in for an emergency landing behind the British lines. The plane bounced across an acre of shell-holes, lost its under-carriage, and finally nosed over on its back. A party of Scottish Highlanders scurried from their trenches to rescue the pilot, who had suffered a broken nose and concussions. A few days later Barker returned to consciousness in a military hospital in Rouen to learn that he had shot down at least six German aircraft – and been awarded the Victoria Cross.

The third Canadian airman to win a VC – and there were only nineteen granted to all British fliers during the four long years of war – was Lieutenant Alan A. McLeod, of Stonewall, Manitoba. McLeod was never lucky enough to fly a single-seater fighter; instead his whole career was spent as the pilot of a slow, awkward Armstrong-Whitworth FK-8, an observation aircraft. But that didn't stop him from attacking zeppelins, enemy airstrips, and German planes that came within machine gun range. In most of these forays his partner in the observer's seat was A.W. Hammond, an Englishman who had already won the Military Cross.

Early in 1918, McLeod and Hammond were set upon by a flight of Fokker triplanes. Again and again they fought off German fighters on their tail, shooting down three or four in the process. Soon the ungainly FK-8 was a sieve of bullet holes. First McLeod was hit, then Hammond, much more severely. But the pilot continued to fly, and the observer propped himself up and kept on firing.

Flames shot back from the engine cowling, enveloping both cockpits – usually the beginning of an end that would leave a curling trail of black smoke across the sky as the plane plunged back to the sullen earth. But McLeod hoisted himself out onto the wing, from where he reached back, alternating hands on the blisteringly hot joy-stick, side-slipping to keep the hungry fire away from Hammond, and somehow managed to get the plane down in one piece, coming to a stop in no man's land, not far from the British trenches.

Hair singed, uniform smouldering, weak from loss of blood, McLeod succeeded in hauling his observer from the burning wreck. Then, encouraged by the shouts of Canadian and Allied soldiers, and protected by the covering fire they laid down, he dragged Hammond from shell-hole to shell-hole until they at last reached the security of the friendly front line.

On May 1, 1918, McLeod was awarded the VC, and Hammond was granted a bar to his Military Cross. On September 4th of that year they appeared together at Buckingham Palace to receive their honours from the King. Tragically, McLeod came down with the Spanish flu a short time later, and died on November 5, 1918 – a mere week before the signing of the Armistice. This magnificent and courageous flier did not live to see either the Allied victory or his own twentieth birthday.

As a group, the Canadians brought down 438 enemy aircraft – and contributed more than 25 per cent of the flying men lost by the RFC during the war. They held eight of the top twenty places among British air aces, including Colonel William Bishop in second place with 72 victories and Major Raymond Collishaw in third place with 68. Captain Donald MacLaren scored 54 victories and Major William Barker 52. Next came Captain G. McElroy with 46, Captain W.G. Claxton with 37, Captain Frank Quigley with 34, and Captain F.R. McCall with 34. It was an impressive record.

The young fighting men of the Dominion left a noble heritage on the western front and wherever they served upon the seas – but nowhere more so than in the live-today, die-tomorrow, nearly virginal skies over France, Belgium and Germany.

Just a name on an honour roll, Flight Commander George Gordon MacLennan was one of the many fighter pilots who lost their lives in aerial combat.

0.3373

CHAPTER NINE

The High Cost of Victory

If it's all the same to history, it need not repeat itself any more.

Bob Edwards, in the *Calgary Eyeopener*, 1919.

In March of 1918 the German high command launched a massive offensive all along the western front. Supported by unprecedented artillery fire, hundreds of thousands of German soldiers poured out across no man's land. It was an all-out attack, designed to bring final victory . . . or final defeat.

By then both sides, battered by the months and years of slaughter, were close to exhaustion. They had given, it seemed, as much as men could be asked to give. And more.

By then, too, the development of the tank had greatly enhanced striking power, nullified the machine gun to some extent, and made it possible for either army to break out of the defensive impasse that had existed since the opening weeks of the war. The invention of an English military historian named Colonel Ernest Swinton, tanks had first been sent into battle by General Haig on the Somme front in September 1916. In the beginning their effectiveness was severely curtailed by their primitive design and a tendency to break down in action. But going into the final year of the war they had been improved sufficiently to assume the role previously played by the cavalry.

And by then the list of engagements in which the Canadians fought and died had lengthened considerably. Behind, for them, lay the dearly-bought glory of Vimy Ridge, Cambrai – where Winnipeg's Fort Garry Horse had spearheaded the attack – and the ghastly human abattoir that was the battle of Passchendaele.

Passchendaele: it is impossible to exaggerate the bestial horror of that hideous nightmare. Men who lived through it had gone in one side of hell and out the other. The terrain – below sea level, soaked by almost continuous rain – was a virtual swamp, the worst site for a major offensive that could have been chosen anywhere along the front. The mud seemed bottomless. Stretcher parties waded hip-deep in it, slogging through the ooze, gaining occasional purchase by stepping on corpses buried in the quagmire. It was incredible that human beings could exist in such conditions, even as pre-historic animals emerging from the slime, let alone fight.

But fight the Canadians did. The travesty went on for almost four months, from August into November, 1917, because General Haig and others of the Allied high command were committed to it. In the end it was the Canadians who led the way into what had been the village of Passchendaele. The gain: a few acres of sterile gumbo, no longer identifiable as a military objective. The cost, in a battle that probably should never have been fought: almost a half-million dead, wounded and

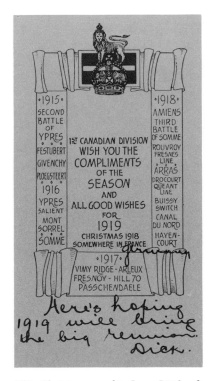

This Christmas card to Lucy Little of Victoria, B.C., was printed and mailed before the armistice of November 11.

Opposite page: *In the summer of 1918 Allied forces smashed through the once impregnable Hindenburg line, and by October Canadian troops had retaken the smouldering city of Cambrai.*

missing Allied soldiers.

Now it was 1918 and through the late spring and into the early summer the awesome German attack swept forward. It rolled past Arras, overcame Cambrai, broke across the Somme, threatened Paris itself. Back home in Canada the realization dawned that the war might actually be lost.

Then, through a combination of indecision on the part of the German high command and the stubborn, magnificent determination of the Canadians and their Allies, the enemy campaign was finally brought to a halt. A stalemate was once again restored. Throughout June and July, as shutters were removed from cottage windows and picnic hampers were brought out of storage back in Canada, it seemed as if there might never be a final act to the marathon tragedy that had been playing in France and Belgium for four uninterrupted years. Perhaps the struggle would just go on and on, exacting its toll forever. Maybe war had become a way of life, something to be accepted and endured as part of the human condition.

the final phase

And then, on August 8, 1918 – later described as "the blackest day in the history of the German army" by General Erich von Ludendorff – the Allied armies, with the battle-hardened Canadian Corps in the vanguard, launched their final counter-attack. The tide had turned. As summer gave way to fall, the Allies, vastly invigorated by the massive transfusion of fresh American troops who stormed out of the Argonne forest behind Verdun, swept north and east toward the German heartland.

There was no stopping them.

Everywhere the enemy fell back, first in orderly withdrawal, then in increasing panic.

It was the final phase of the war.

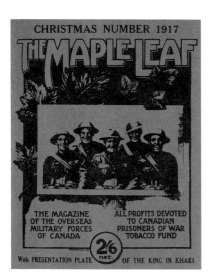

CHRISTMAS NUMBER 1917
THE MAPLE LEAF

THE MAGAZINE OF THE OVERSEAS MILITARY FORCES OF CANADA — ALL PROFITS DEVOTED TO CANADIAN PRISONERS OF WAR TOBACCO FUND

2/6 net.

With PRESENTATION PLATE OF THE KING IN KHAKI

The Maple Leaf *was one of a handful of magazines printed overseas for a bit of comic relief. Caricatures of Germans always got a laugh, but most of the fun-poking was directed at the naive recruit and the bully officer.*

In the last hundred days, from August to November, the Canadian Corps suffered an additional 16,000 casualties; but it played a major role in the British advance that destroyed fifty German divisions.

the eleventh hour

By then Currie's soldiers, who had come from their cities, towns and farms with no military heritage to call upon, were battle-hardened veterans with a reputation for great striking power and a tradition of always taking their objective. Lloyd George would later write in his memoirs:

The Canadians played a part of such distinction . . . that thenceforth they were marked out as storm troops; for the remainder of the war they were brought along to head the assault in one great battle after another. Whenever the Germans found the Canadian Corps coming into the line, they prepared for the worst.

The Allied armies continued to press home their advantage. Cambrai, Douai and Mons were added to the list of place names that would soon be engraved on war memorials in parks all across Canada. France was liberated. Then Belgium. The great assault surged forward, spilling toward the frontiers of Germany.

On November 8, 1918 – a bleak, grey day with low, sombre clouds and the threat of snow in the air – French Field Marshal Foch received a German Armistice Commission in a coach of his special train, on a siding near the forest of Compiègne. A coal-fire hissed and flared against the external cold and the chill formalities of military and diplomatic protocol.

Three days later, at a pre-dawn ceremony in that same railway coach, the formal surrender terms were signed. Shortly afterward Canadian Brigade Headquarters received a message, which began: "Hostilities will cease at 11 A.M., November 11th, 1918 . . ."

Just after eight o'clock, when the breakfast tea was being brewed and the early winter sun was beginning to slant across the battle fields, the long-awaited word spread through the Canadian trenches like a prairie grass fire. It was, by and large, received calmly. There was still almost three hours to go, and more than one Canadian soldier would die in that short, anti-climactic span. Then, at eleven o'clock, the guns fell silent and an incredible stillness descended over the western front. A soldier from New Glasgow, Nova Scotia, remembers that he heard a bird singing, and wondered how it could possibly have survived.

It was late morning or early afternoon (depending on the time zone) when the news, flashed across the Atlantic by wireless, reached Canada. It had been expected for several days, but when it came at last the confirmation that the war was finally over touched off an emotional outpouring that spread from Atlantic to Pacific. People laughed, cried, shouted, danced, kissed strangers. There was an incredible feeling of relief. There were prayers of gratitude. There was swelling pride. And, for many, there was the bittersweet awareness that their boy would never be coming home again.

impromptu parades

The glorious word reached Edmonton at 2 P.M. All over the city factory whistles blew, church bells peeled, fire department sirens wailed. Work came to a complete stop. Impromptu parades clogged the streets.

In Vancouver, twenty-five thousand people congregated around the corner of Granville and Hastings Streets. All the boats in the harbour blew their whistles. That afternoon there was a monster parade. Horns tooted, bagpipes skirled, fireworks

The smiles and shouts of this truckload of "Tommies" say only one thing – VICTORY. On Nov. 11, 1918, Canadian forces recaptured Mons, the city where the British first saw action four years before.

Homecoming

Even though the war was over, it was many months before the first troops returned. Details of the armistice provided for occupation of the Rhineland by the Canadian Corps until February. Nearly 4,000 men of the CEF serving in Siberia waited until April before their orders home came through. And even those men who were billetted in England had to wait for months while American and Canadian leaders squabbled over priority on ships ready to cross the Atlantic. Eventually the war vets did return, and festivities that had marked the victory were rekindled.

Boys and girls who had grown up during the war welcomed their fathers and brothers home to Edmonton.

These women of Fenelon Falls, Ont., celebrated the victory and reunion with a costume pageant titled "Hands Across the Border," showing all the flags of the Allied countries.

exploded, patients from the military hospital were driven through the streets in decorated cars, waving to the cheering throngs.

In Kingston, Ontario, crowds gathered to read the bulletins posted by the *Whig-Standard*. Later, factories and stores closed, and school children were let out early so that everyone could attend a great victory celebration in the city park.

an invasion of influenza

In Regina thousands roamed the streets, laughing, shouting, dragging effigies of the German Kaiser behind their cars. Afterward most of the population trooped out to Wascana Park to listen to speeches by municipal and provincial dignitaries and sing war songs. As the early dusk gathered, farmers who had been forbidden to burn straw-stacks during the war set them alight, adding a glow to the skies that could be seen for miles.

It was much the same everywhere – in Montreal and Moose Jaw, in Pilot Mound and Peggy's Cove, in New Liskeard and New Westminster.

It was finally over, over there.

But the decade of agony was far from ready to forsake its hegemony over the people of the Dominion. In the last three months of 1918, Canada, along with most of the world, was hit by the worst epidemic since the Black Death of the Middle Ages, an invasion of the dreaded influenza virus known as the Spanish 'flu. By the time the Armistice was signed, the whole country was in its grasp. And it was at least as deadly, and as chillingly impersonal, as shrapnel fire.

Hospitals, their wards filled to overflowing, had to turn thousands away. Undertakers and casket-makers could not keep up with the demand. Something like one in every four people in Canada contracted the disease.

In Regina all church services, public meetings and mass entertainments were banned. Schools were converted into temporary hospitals. Streetcars were disinfected nightly. Anyone coughing, sneezing or spitting in public was liable to a $50 fine.

The first cases were reported in Edmonton on October 19; by the end of the month 2,000 had fallen victim and 44 were dead. The Alberta Board of Health ordered everyone to wear gauze masks in public. Stores and businesses were forbidden to open until 12:30 each day. Pembina Hall at the University of Alberta became an emergency centre. By November 11, the toll had risen to 262 dead.

In Montreal stores were told to close at 4 P.M.

In Hamilton a department store announced that there would be no Santa Claus that year.

In Peterborough, Ontario so many doctors and nurses had themselves fallen ill that there was a critical shortage of medical aid.

In Toronto many barbers closed down their shops, and those who remained open wore surgical masks in a vain attempt to keep out the germs.·

a bizarre variety of cures

Medical authorities were almost powerless to treat the disease, or keep it from spreading, and people turned in desperation to a bizarre variety of home cures and preventatives. Everyone stopped shaking hands, and most swore off kissing. Many ate raw onions and garlic. Others inhaled fumes from hot water and turpentine. A few favoured poultices of cooked onions worn around the neck. Some drank concoctions of warm milk, ginger, soda, sugar and black pepper.

Nothing really worked, and the epidemic continued its inexorable rampage through that Christmas, the winter months that followed, and into the first days of spring when, according to some mysterious pattern, it began to peter out.

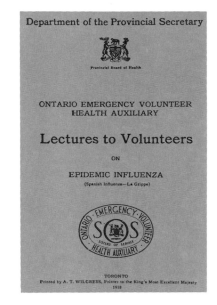

Department of the Provincial Secretary

Provincial Board of Health

ONTARIO EMERGENCY VOLUNTEER HEALTH AUXILIARY

Lectures to Volunteers

ON

EPIDEMIC INFLUENZA
(Spanish Influenza—La Grippe)

TORONTO
Printed by A. T. WILGRESS, Printer to the King's Most Excellent Majesty
1918

As if the war had not taken enough of its toll in fatalities, in the winter of 1918 North America was hit by the worst epidemic since the horrific Black Death of the Middle Ages. Men, women and children wore gauze masks at home, at work and in public places; the acrid stench of formaldehyde and other disinfectants hung in the air; people fumigated houses, schools and offices, but it was all futile. Before the disease had run its course, 65,000 Canadians had died of "Spanish 'flu."

Keep Them Smiling

Soldiers Home Coming Campaign

The Salvation Army Million Dollar Fund

January 19th to 25th

"FIRST TO SERVE—LAST TO APPEAL"

THE SALVATION ARMY MILLION DOLLAR FUND COMMITTEE

Headquarters: 20 Albert St., Toronto

[1919]

The Salvation Army's million dollar fund was one of several campaigns to ease the soldier's return to civilian life. While the "Sally Anns" tried to keep them smiling, governments and private business worried over jobs for the veterans.

By March 1919, the Spanish 'flu had killed almost 65,000 Canadians, more than had died in Europe. Montreal recorded 3,128 deaths. Toronto lost over 1,600. Ottawa had suffered 570 'flu losses. In Alberta some 30,000 had caught the disease, and one in every ten had died from it. These were ghastly figures to be added to the terrible toll of the years of agony overseas.

disembarking at Halifax

And that toll was sombre, indeed. According to the final compilations, arrived at some years later, 8,538,315 soldiers, sailors and airmen of all nations had died in the Great War, plus an additional 7,750,919 captured or missing and 21,219,452 wounded – and these totals did not include civilian casualties, which were substantial.

In terms of population, the Dominion had paid more than its proportionate price. Close to 60,000 Canadians were dead in what was then optimistically called "the war to end all wars." One in eight Canadian men of military age had become a casualty – killed, missing in action, or wounded. Tens of thousands would live on in veterans' hospitals for forty, fifty, sixty years – amputees, human vegetables, men with their lungs destroyed by gas attacks, remembered only in dutiful visits by next of kin and during the two-minute silence each November 11, when buglers blew the "Last Post," and their comrades-in-arms stood around war memorials from Prince Edward Island to British Columbia, growing a little more portly each year, their medals clanging against the stiff, freshly-pressed lapels of their blue serge suits.

It was late winter, 1919, before the boys began to come home, often returning on the same troop ships that had taken them overseas three or four years earlier, disembarking at Halifax, which still bore the scars of the 1917 explosion, then fanning out across the country on special trains. By then

they had endured months of frustrating, boring demobilization procedures to satisfy the clerks and accountants and scribes, and once or twice they had vented their impatience by rioting at various camps in England. Civilian troops are always quick to enlist, and equally quick to demand their discharges once the crisis is passed.

Finally, between January and May, 1919, they returned – hardened, battle-tempered soldiers who had so recently been tender boys, ordinary fathers and men without jobs. They marched up the main streets of their cities, towns and villages, while the drums rolled and the bagpipes skirled – full of pride, but terribly aware of how long they had been away, how much they had missed, all the things that had changed, and the missing ranks of their friends who had not survived to relish that day.

It was a scene that was to be repeated a hundred, a thousand times, as when Nova Scotia's famous regiment, the Twenty-Fifth, marched along Barrington Street to be welcomed at a ceremony at Government House. The ranks of the fabled Royal Canadians marched proudly, but contained no more than a dozen men who had gone overseas almost four years earlier.

to welcome the warriors home

One such return in Edmonton was typical of scenes across the country:

In the forenoon of March 22, four years less one month since the battalion had left Edmonton, 30,000 citizens lined Jasper Ave. and crowded down to the CPR station to watch the 49th come home. Admission to the station and the platform had been restricted to the Next-of-Kin Association, while along the approaches to the station a thousand veterans were drawn up. Waiting to welcome the warriors were Lieutenant-Governor

Brett, Premier Charles Stewart, Mayor Joe Clarke, Bishop Gray, and many other clerics and dignitaries . . . .

As the first train, rumbling over the High Level Bridge came in sight, clacked over the Jasper Ave. overpass, and hissed to a stop, the 49th [had] returned . . . .

Eventually, with the crowd falling in behind it, the battalion marched east through the crowds lining Jasper Ave., turned onto 101 St., then west again to the armouries. There, for the last time, the battalion was 'dismissed.'

a well-remembered face

There were many, of course, who did not, could not share in the homecoming festivities: those whose loved ones would never return. Fathers who took off storm-windows or shoveled snow from walks, instead of going down to the railway station to watch eagerly for the first glimpse of a well-remembered face. Mothers who made themselves busy in their kitchens, and tried not to think of the rooms upstairs that would never be used again. Young widows who would sleep alone that night, as they had for so many months and would for so many years. Little children who played in the leaves of the previous fall, or sat in classrooms, or lay in bed at night, and tried without success to remember what their fathers had looked like.

By the late spring of 1919 what was left of the Canadian Corps, the whole and the un-whole, were back on their native soil.

What they had returned to, drastically changed from what they had left, would be revealed in the weeks, months and years that lay ahead.

The Unknown Soldier

Somewhere in Canada, on a dresser or mantle, this photograph occupied a place of honour. Nothing is known of the three brothers who, each in a different branch of the service, lived through some of the years of agony. Was this moment in the photographer's studio one of the last they shared? Or did they return home and pick up the pieces of a life they had hardly known?

The Art of Tom Thomson

He was the most unusually talented artist Canada had yet produced. He was an expert outdoorsman and canoeist, was usually broke, and never married. When war broke out and his fellow painters – men who we now know as "the Group of Seven" – enlisted to fight in a foreign war, an unnecessary war, he thought, he fled to the wilds of Northern Ontario. When they learned that he was dead, "drowned" said the autopsy report, they felt more than the loss of a friend. To them he was a genius, an artist who, in Arthur Lismer's words, expressed moods "while the rest of us were painting pictures." He loved the rough and ragged country of the Canadian Shield and saw a magnificence there that had never before been captured. Tom Thomson's body was found on July 16, 1917 at Canoe Lake, some days after his death. Was it murder (his feet were tangled in fishing line), or was it suicide? – we may never know. However, we do know that the effect of Thomson's work on Canadian painting has been immeasureable.

A great artist, and an expert fly-fisherman.

The West Wind *(1917), one of a few large paintings he completed after sketching in Algonquin Park.*

This poetic panel (1916) has a hint of Thomson's later style.

The Pool *(c. 1915), and other paintings from the same year show Thomson pushing his style to the edge of abstraction and his palette to the limits of vividness and colour.*

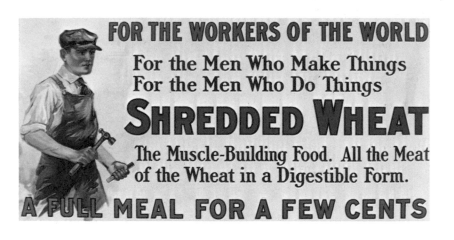

FOR THE WORKERS OF THE WORLD

For the Men Who Make Things
For the Men Who Do Things

SHREDDED WHEAT

The Muscle-Building Food. All the Meat of the Wheat in a Digestible Form.

A FULL MEAL FOR A FEW CENTS

THE WORLD IS HERS
if she knows

SHREDDED WHEAT

and the many wholesome, nourishing dishes that can be made with it. Ready-cooked, ready-to-serve, no kitchen worry. No servant problem. Combines deliciously with all kinds of fruit.

FOR THE DESK-MAN

For the Man Who Plans
For the Man Who Directs

SHREDDED WHEAT

Keeps the Brain Clear and the Bowels Healthy and Active.

EAT IT FOR BREAKFAST OR LUNCH

FOR THE HOME-MAKER

For the Woman in the Factory in the Store, or in the Office

SHREDDED WHEAT

is the Perfect Food.
All the Meat of the Wheat.

READY—COOKED   READY—TO—EAT

No Worry, No Hurry
in the home where

SHREDDED WHEAT

is served for breakfast. It is ready-cooked, ready-to-serve. The top-notch breakfast cereal–always clean, always pure, always the same.

DELICIOUS WITH FRESH OR STEWED FRUITS

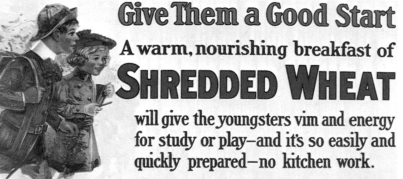

Give Them a Good Start

A warm, nourishing breakfast of

SHREDDED WHEAT

will give the youngsters vim and energy for study or play–and it's so easily and quickly prepared–no kitchen work.

READY-COOKED AND READY-TO-EAT

CHAPTER TEN

The Aftermath

There are those in Winnipeg who think the shooting on Saturday taught labour a lesson. But labour did not need the lesson. . . .

J.S. Woodsworth, on Winnipeg General Strike, 1919.

The war had produced an economic boom, and a phenomenal growth in industry. By the time it ended 586,000 workers – about one-third of them women – were employed in manufacturing. The gross national product increased by two and a half times between 1914 and 1918. Steel production, artificially inflated by the demand for munitions, leaped from one million to two and a quarter million ingot tons. Almost everybody who could work had a job.

The return of peace caused a short-lived but acute upheaval. To help cushion the transition some war-time plants continued production for a time, but others closed their doors almost before the ink on the peace treaties was dry. In some areas – mining, for example – demand was suddenly reduced drastically or dried up altogether, and large numbers of employees were laid off.

The effect of such cut-backs was compounded by the simultaneous re-entry into the labour market of hundreds of thousands of returnees from overseas. The result, by 1920, was widespread unemployment – and considerable disillusionment among veterans who had returned as heroes, only to find that society seemed to have no place for

them. In Vancouver, for example, many of "the boys" had to resign themselves to whiling away their days on the park benches in "Victory Squares," and rehashing their war experiences.

Those who did find work discovered that wages were good compared to before the war, but that prices had leaped ahead in even longer bounds. In Edmonton the cost of living had shot up by 58 per cent since 1914. Across the country and around the world, a shortage of peace-time goods led to further inflation. In Montreal men's winter coats, available for $5 in the fall of 1914, cost $13.95 in the winter of 1918. Round steak was up from 10 to 39 cents a pound. Coffee had more than doubled in price. There had been little building during the war, and many cities experienced a serious housing shortage, with resulting high rents.

Returning veterans were surprised by a number of other changes. One was a dramatic increase in the number of cars on the road. In 1914, when there were only some 80,000 licensed owners, the horseless carriage had still been something of a curiosity; but by 1919 there were 277,000 motor vehicles, and cities like Calgary, where automobile registration had increased tenfold in less than a decade, were experiencing their first rush-hour traffic jams.

The bars and saloons were gone, and if a man wanted a drink he had either to arrange to have a "prescription" filled by a sympathetic druggist or

Prohibition came to Quebec in 1919. Anyone wanting to buy alcohol (for medicinal purposes only, of course!) had to pay the 20¢ tax per bottle.

Opposite page: It's a woman's world; it's a worker's world; it's a desk man's world; it's a homemaker's world. The war years had brought about a lot of changes, and the ad men at Shredded Wheat used them all to sell cereal.

**Emily Murphy
"Janey Canuck"**

Raised in a family with a history in law reform and politics, it is no wonder that Emily Murphy made such an impact on the fight for women's rights. She was born in Cookstown, Ontario in 1868 and was educated at Bishop Strachan School in Toronto. She married at nineteen and after spending two years abroad came back to Toronto where she published her first of six books, *Janey Canuck Abroad* (1901), a vivid description of England's urban slums. In 1904 the Murphys moved out to Manitoba and finally settled in Edmonton where "Janey" campaigned for women's property rights, the establishment of family courts and a greater participatory role for women in politics. Her interest in social justice led to her appointment in 1916 as the first woman police magistrate in Canada and the empire.

visit a bootlegger's joint.

Those soldiers who got home early witnessed some of the results of the emancipation women had achieved during the war – including the right to vote, an acknowledged role as wage-earners and greatly increased freedom to dress as they saw fit. A few women, and not just streetwalkers, actually smoked cigarettes in public! But 1919 fashions featured a return of floor-length skirts from the rising hemlines of the war years, a change which may have symbolized an almost tacit return to subordinate status on the part of Canadian women.

a kaleidoscopic mix

In most ways, of course, peace-time living turned out to be much as it had been prior to 1914 – a kaleidoscopic mix of the routine and monotonous, relieved by occasional glints of pleasure, and high-lighted now and again by out-of-the-ordinary events.

New hit tunes like "I'm Always Chasing Rainbows" and "After You've Gone" replaced the poignant ballads of the war years.

The movie houses did good business; some — like the Regent on Toronto's Adelaide St. — had full pit orchestras instead of anonymous pianists to back up their silent films. But people were impatient for the advent of the "talkies," which were rumoured to be at hand.

One of the most popular theatrical attractions was The Dumbells, a troupe originally pulled together to entertain the Canadian soldiers before the terrible battle of Vimy Ridge. Under the direction of Captain Merton Plunkett, The Dumbells were already a smash success in London's Coliseum and a hit on New York's Broadway. Featuring such stars as Red Newman ("Oh, It's a Lovely War"), Pat Rafferty and Fred Emney, the troupe played to overflow audiences in cities and towns from Charlottetown to Victoria.

Sports leagues welcomed the return of many of their star athletes, and donated trophies and unveiled plaques to those who had played their final games several thousand miles from home.

The war had brought about a great advance in the technology of radio, and a few pioneer stations in the United States – KDKA, Pittsburgh, and WGY, Schenectady, New York – were broadcasting several hours of words and music each day. As one of the first recognitions of the new electronic age, the Marconi Wireless Telegraph Company in Halifax offered a few receiver parts for sale in the windows of its Granville Street office.

The art world was agog over the strange death of Tom Thomson in Algonquin Park, and bitterly divided as to the merits of his confreres, including war artists Frederick Varley and A.Y. Jackson, who were shortly to become famous as members of "The Group of Seven." Some saw their work as reflecting a particular Canadian genius; others saw it as undisciplined hen scratching.

aviation grows up

One of the major social events of 1919 was the mid-summer visit of Edward, Prince of Wales, the heir to the British throne. Canadian veterans remembered that the Prince, still wearing war-time khaki, had visited their trenches and shared with them the horrors of the western front. Handsome though shy, he made debutante hearts beat faster when he appeared at a dance at Toronto's Royal Canadian Yacht Club. And when he left on August 27, 50,000 Torontonians lined his route to bid him fond adieu.

Although still only in its early adolescence, aviation had grown up considerably during the war years. At the 1918 Canadian National Exhibition in Toronto a woman aviator named Ruth Law had raced against an automobile – and lost. And in that same year the country's first airmail service

Prince Charming

When Prince Edward took Canada by storm in August 1919, it was not just another royal tour – far from it. The war was over, Canadians had sacrificed more than anyone had expected, and it was time for an official "thanks." From the moment he stepped ashore, Edward captivated the crowds and press. He broke with royal traditions and covered what even the King and Queen thought were *faux pas* with his famous smile. He jumped on a horse at the Calgary Stampede and showed the cowboys how to ride; he danced with the same girl *nine* times at a Hamilton party; and insisted on talking to grimy stevedores on the Halifax docks. Young women were thrilled, but their elders clucked disapproval. This was no way for proper royalty to behave!

The adventurous prince and WW I ace Billy Barker, before the two take a spin.

Movie cameras roll and press cameras click as the 25-year-old prince endures the official ceremonies and pouring rain at his arrival in St. John, N.B.

had been inaugurated between the Ontario capital and Montreal.

In the fall of 1919 the country thrilled to The Great Toronto-New York Air Race, a promotion sponsored by the Canadian National Exhibition. Entered was an astonishing collection of planes and pilots. The aircraft ranged from antiquated pre-war crates to military trainers to surplus Sopwith Camels and Spads, late of the western front. The men who flew them included super-ace Billy Barker, VC; C.A. "Duke" Schiller, who would soon become one of Canada's most colourful and most successful frontier pilots; and "Shorty" Schroeder, an American destined to earn fame as an explorer in the rarefied atmosphere of high altitude flying.

the bush-flying saga begins

The Great Race turned out to be a hilarious adventure. One pilot, hopelessly lost, landed in Windsor, Ontario. Another plunged into Lake Ontario, and was rescued thanks to the inflated inner-tube he was carrying. A third, blinded by the smoke-pot set out to show him the wind direction, stripped the harness from a horse and buggy with his wing tip, but landed without damage to either animal or aircraft. Miraculously, no one was killed.

"You could follow the course easily" Duke Schiller recalled later, "just by keeping an eye open for the wreckage along the way."

Shorty Schroeder eventually wobbled in for a landing at Toronto's Leaside airdrome, and was proclaimed the winner.

At the same time, other veterans of the Royal Flying Corps were writing the first paragraphs in the saga of bush-flying. Pioneer flying operations were set up in many cities. In Regina, for example, Roland Groome and Ed Clarke, two Canadian pilots who had served with the RFC, bought a

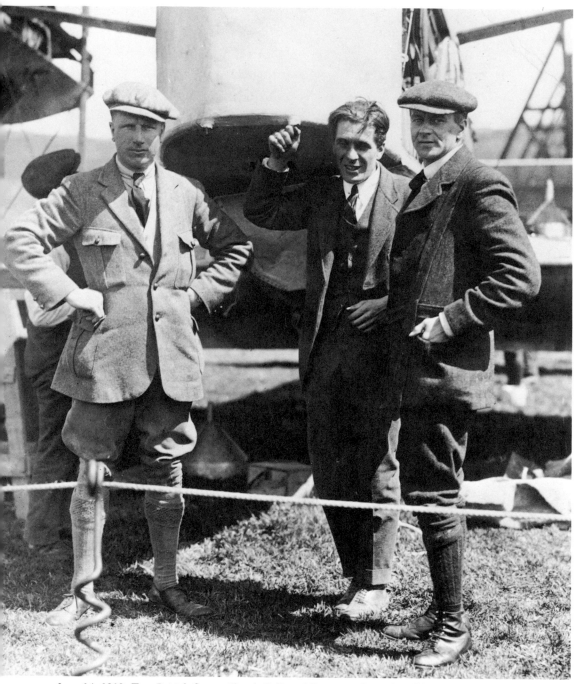

June 14, 1919: Two British flyers, Alcock (left) and Brown (right), take off from Newfoundland attempting to cross the Atlantic non-stop. They crash-land in an Irish bog 16 hours later and make history.

116

Curtiss biplane and established a primitive airdrome on the prairie not far from the legislative building. In Edmonton "Wop" May and his brother Court organized May Airplanes Ltd., rented a Curtiss JN4, and arranged with a district farmer to take off and land in his pasture field, where they built a crude hangar. As a promotional stunt to drum up business, May often flew under the High Level Bridge over the river, and once, with Mayor Joe Clarke as a passenger, swooped down over Ross Flats Field so that his honour could throw out the first ball to open the baseball season. A second Edmonton airline operation, headed by Captain Keith Tailyour, inaugurated regular flights to the Peace River country in 1919.

On the international scene Borden was waging a long, hard, and ultimately successful struggle to gain adequate Canadian representation at the Paris Peace Conference and later at the founding of the League of Nations. Through his efforts, supported by Jan Christian Smuts of South Africa, the dominions were finally allowed to send two delegates each to the peace conference – and, as still more significant progress – to sign the peace treaty separately. (Until then Great Britain would have signed on behalf of the empire as a whole.)

an independent voice

The torch had to be taken up again when Canada's right to seek election to the Council of the League of Nations was challenged. In an angry letter to Lloyd George, Borden delivered a ringing declaration that Canada would not accept an inferior position in the international arena:

The Dominions have maintained their place before the world during the past five years through sacrifices which no nation outside of Europe has known. I am confident that the people of Canada will not tamely submit to a dictation which declares that Liberia or Cuba, Panama or Hedjaz, Haiti or Ecuador, must have a higher place . . . than can be accorded to their own country.

But, while Canada was gaining an independent voice in the council chambers of the world, based largely on her impressive – and, to external eyes, united – efforts during the war, there was disquieting evidence of deep conflicts in the domestic structure of the Dominion that was strung out along the sturdy spine of the great Pre-Cambrian Shield.

growing disenchantment

The conscription crisis of 1917 and the wartime election had left a legacy of increased bitterness between Quebec and the rest of the country.

There was also growing disenchantment and unrest among the farmers of the nation, particularly from the Lakehead to the foothills of the Rockies. Among wheat growers, increased costs – wages, the price of land, farm machinery, fertilizer – seemed to have outstripped grain prices. During the war years they had been willing to work long hours under very difficult conditions to fulfil their roles as custodians of the "bread-basket" of the western, Allied world. Now, with the coming of peace, was the time of reckoning.

There was resentment against war-time profiteering in the cities, strong opposition to the high freight rates charged on goods coming in from the industrial east, and a new surge of support for reciprocity with the United States. The situation was aggravated by the fact that prairie crops were drastically short in both 1917 and 1918, due to droughts which caused the first serious soil erosion and presaged the infamous Dust Bowl of the 1930s.

The farmers and their spokesmen were prepared to take political action. In 1916, the Canadi-

CANADIAN NATIONAL EXHIBITION

—TORONTO—

Aug. 28 – Sept. 11

"The Greatest Annual Event on Earth"

100 buildings—264 acres of beautiful grounds—1 mile of waterfront.

"The Empire Triumphant"

Magnificent pageant of color, light and action—1500 performers. A well-spring of patriotic inspiration.

Incomparable music—two score bands.

Daily demonstration by Northwest Mounted Police.

Aug. 28 - Automobile Racing - Aug. 30

Cols. Bishop and Barker, and other world-famed pilots, in daily aeroplane flights and fights.

Mile-a-minute Motor Boats.

Electrical Show—National Motor Show—America's Best Live Stock, Poultry, Tractor, Farm Machinery, Dog and Cat Shows—Government Exhibits and Demonstrations. And a score of other special attractions.

Consult railways for fares and information.

JOHN G. KENT, Gen. Mgr.

Tucked into this extravaganza program of the CNE are three crowd pleasers: auto races, mile-a-minute motor boats, and aerobatics by Bishop and Barker.

FARM BUILDINGS AND EQUIPMENT

SOLDIERS' LAND SETTLEMENT SCHEME

This Booklet contains official plans and drawings of buildings which have been designed by the Settlement Board for Soldier Settlers only.

Suggestions are also given for four different Soldier Equipments:—

No. 1 - One-Man Equipment.
No. 2 - Two or Three-Man Equipment.
No. 3 - Man, Wife and Small Family Equipment.
No. 4 - Man, Wife and Larger Family Equipment.

THE T. EATON CO. LIMITED
WINNIPEG   CANADA

Finding jobs for returning soldiers and immigrants was no small problem. War industries were shutting down and city work was hard to get. One scheme for taking up the employment slack was to encourage settlement in the West, and both government and business tried to make the proposition as appealing and easy (and lucrative) as possible.

an Council of Agriculture, claiming to represent primary producers from coast to coast, came into being. Within four years it was to spawn the National Progressive Party, led by Thomas A. Crerar, a Manitoba Liberal who had resigned as Minister of Agriculture in Borden's Union Government. Meanwhile regional farmers' parties were rising to prominence, and one, the United Farmers of Ontario, scored a dramatic victory in the 1919 election in that province.

an alliance of workers

Country versus city – it was an ancient antagonism. But it took on increasing sharpness and bitterness in the gathering atmosphere of confrontation that spread across the Canadian nation in the year or two following the victory on the western front.

During the war, labour union membership had more than doubled as circumstances had created an employees' market. Men and women were no longer just grateful to have jobs; they were more and more inclined to join together in demanding adequate pay and safe, decent working conditions in exchange for their labours. With the return of peace the unions became increasingly militant and much more radical, especially in the west. Although almost all of the leaders were primarily influenced by the British labour movement, there was also a heady awareness of the proletarian revolution that had swept across Russia in 1917 and 1918. Merchants, industrialists and other capitalists were understandably shaken by statements such as that published in the *Western Labour News* in January, 1919: "When the workers take control they will form a Dictatorship which will give the same order to the owners . . . that Lenin gave to the former owners of Russia: obey or starve!"

In May of that year the largest labour meeting

ever held in western Canada packed Calgary's Paget Hall. The mood of the 239 delegates was confident, truculent and loudly responsive to the "action now" demands of one speaker after another. Out of the meeting came an endorsement of the idea of One Big Union – a nation-wide alliance of all workers, regardless of trades, to confront big business with a solid front. The O.B.U. accepted Karl Marx' concept of the class struggle as a basic tenet, and saw the general strike as the most effective weapon available to working men. When the delegates departed they were committed to seek the support of their own unions for the O.B.U., and for a coast-to-coast strike of all union members to begin on the first of June.

But before they could get home, Winnipeg had jumped the gun. The confrontation that was to shake the Dominion began with two separate walk-outs – one by the city's metal workers, the other by those engaged in the building trades. Appealed to for support, the Winnipeg Trades and Labour Council called for a general sympathy strike among all unions, a proposal that won almost unanimous endorsement, by 11,000 to 500 votes.

joining the exodus

The massive shut-down began at 11 o'clock on the morning of May 15, 1919. Within two hours the city was almost completely paralyzed. Clerks, teamsters, bakers, printers, electricians, caretakers, carpenters, tailors, blacksmiths walked off their jobs. The streetcars stopped running. The postal workers hit the bricks. Factories, offices and stores emptied. Firemen in Winnipeg and neighbouring St. Boniface booked off. Waterworks employees joined the exodus, leaving skeleton crews at the pumping stations to maintain minimum pressure. The Winnipeg police force voted overwhelming support for the strike, but agreed to stay on duty in the interests of law and order.

The Winnipeg Trades and Labour Council had called out its entire membership of 12,000 but soon discovered that at least twice, and perhaps three times that number, caught up in the strike fever, had walked off their jobs.

to restore law and order

Within the next couple of days it became obvious that control had passed from city hall to the strike committee and its headquarters in room 10 of the Labour Temple on North Main Street. There was plenty of intelligence and administrative talent available there to get the job done – including John Queen, who would later serve seven terms as mayor of Winnipeg; J.S. Woodsworth, who became the founder of the CCF party in 1932; and A.A. Heaps, who held a seat in the House of Commons from 1925 to 1940. By and large the city was served well by such men, who operated under conditions of extreme difficulty.

Meanwhile, most middle- and upper-class citizens, partly influenced by the two Winnipeg newspapers, the *Free Press* and the *Tribune,* tended to see the strike as a Bolshevik plot to take over the city, and later the country. "To all practical purposes" the *Tribune* editorialized, "Winnipeg is now under the Soviet system of government."

Soon a Citizens' Committee of One Thousand was organized under the direction of A.K. Godfrey, a grain and lumber merchant. With its headquarters in the Board of Trade Building, the Citizens' Committee, largely composed of business and professional men, and predictably reactionary, set out to restore vital services – including bread and milk deliveries, mail, fire protection, water pressure, daily newspapers.

Mayor Charles Gray, Premier T.C. Norris and Prime Minister Robert Borden all pledged themselves to the task of restoring law and order in

The War Measures Act of 1914 restricted travel outside the country. Before it was lifted in 1919, Edward Maile, a discharged soldier turned salesman, needed this permit to cross into the U.S.

Headlines from Western Labour News, the clarion of Winnipeg's Trades and Labour Council, outline the events and attitudes that surrounded the General Strike of the summer of 1919. The first signs of unrest brewing in labour's ranks showed in the spring of 1918 when union leaders from the West rejected the moderate platform of the TLC, tabled at Quebec, and decided to organize for a show of strength.

Winnipeg. A squadron of North West Mounted Police, returning from overseas, was ordered to detrain at the Manitoba capital. Militia units were called out and given special training. Crates of machine guns and other armaments were shipped in, bearing labels of "Regimental Baggage." Adherents of the Committee of One Thousand were sworn in as special police.

"Bloody Saturday"

Meanwhile, many of the returned veterans had taken sides in the dispute. Most supported the strikers, and paraded to the skirl of bagpipes and the roll of drums, battle-hardened soldiers who thoroughly alarmed the city's wealthier citizens. But others, so recently brothers-in-arms, and equally familiar with violence, joined the Soldiers' Loyalist Association and pledged themselves to break the strike at whatever cost.

And so, in an atmosphere of accelerating bitterness, the city was divided into two armed camps.

On June 6 the mayor banned all parades, assemblies and demonstrations. Three days later all but fifteen members of the police force were dismissed because they refused to abdicate their right to strike, and replaced by "special constables" – vigilantes approved by the Committee of One Thousand.

On that day, June 9, a skirmish broke out on downtown streets between the strikers and Mounties and special constables which resulted in several injuries and a number of arrests.

Some days later, in the early, pre-dawn hours of the morning, a force of fifty mounted policemen and almost five hundred special constables descended on the homes of the strike leaders, and arrested some of them. They were shortly released on bail, but not before working-class indignation had been fanned to prairie grass-fire heat.

About noon on June 21, the day shortly to be immortalized as "Bloody Saturday," thousands of strikers and strike-supporters congregated along Main Street just north of Portage Avenue. Their mood was belligerent, defiant, surly, perhaps even ugly, but they were not out for violence. They were looking for a direction, a sign, and it was not long in appearing.

Public transportation had been partially restored by then, and a southbound streetcar came, clanging its bell, along Main Street. The mob closed around it, bringing it to a halt. Someone *was* pulled off the trolley. Others swarmed aboard, the motorman fled and the few terrified passengers scampered to safety. Windows were smashed, cushions torn apart, seats ripped out. Moments later flames leaped up and oily, black smoke drifted over the scene.

Suddenly the clatter of hoof beats on bricks and pavement came from the direction of Portage Avenue, and waves of scarlet-and-khaki Mounties came charging north on Main Street. The mob fell back, shouting defiance, some hurling stones and bottles. The mounted policemen flailed away with clubs until their horses were stopped by the sheer mass of demonstrators.

"Those are real bullets!"

In the midst of the wild confusion Mayor Gray read the Riot Act from the steps of city hall, but few could hear the solemn words.

The Mounties regrouped and attacked once more, this time brandishing pistols instead of truncheons. "My God," a bystander shouted in disbelief, "those are real bullets! They're shooting to kill!" A man named Mike Sokolowski fell to the ground in front of the Manitoba Hotel, a bullet through his heart. Another, Steven Schezerbanowes, shot in both legs, would die later of gangrene. Several dozen demonstrators, trapped in

Bloody Saturday

On May 15, 1919, 2,000 workers in metal trades in Winnipeg walked off their jobs. Their demands: a minimum wage of 85¢ an hour, a 44-hour week, and the right to collective bargaining. Within one week 33,000 others had joined their ranks. All essential services closed down and the city was paralyzed. City government leaders and the white-collar "Citizens' Committee of 1,000" saw the action as part of an international Bolshevik conspiracy that had to be snuffed out. On June 21, "Bloody Saturday," special police and Mounties carrying baseball bats and loaded guns broke up a protest parade.

The General Strike divided Winnipeg's population under labour and "law and order" banners.

Striking workers volunteered to "man" essential services.

Mounties and uniformed ex-servicemen restored law and order after six hours of bloody confrontation.

a dead-end street, later to be dubbed "Hell's Alley," were beaten to the ground and trampled by the horses.

A convoy of cars and trucks, loaded with soldiers with fixed bayonets and some machine guns, made its way through the milling crowd, but by then the fighting was all but over. Soon the strikers and their supporters began to drift away, and by late afternoon Main Street was deserted except for military patrols.

As night fell ninety-one persons were in jail, and thirty were in hospitals, including six Mounted Police officers and two city police constables who had been thrown from a roof.

The spirit of the workers had been crushed by the bloodshed, and by the obvious determination of the authorities to use whatever force might be necessary to maintain order. To all intents and purposes the Winnipeg General Strike was over, although it would not end officially until the following Wednesday, June 25.

trials followed with interest

The trials of the strike leaders which took place over the next few months were followed with tremendous interest all across Canada. The crown claimed that eight men – John Queen, A.A. Heaps, William Ivens, Fred Dixon, R.B. Russell, R.J. Johns, R.E. Bray and William Pritchard – had, among other things, joined in a conspiracy to bring about a Soviet form of government in Canada. After lengthy sittings that were often as stormy as any ever held in Canada, they were convicted of a variety of offences and sentenced to terms of from six months to two years.

Viewed calmly, the evidence seemed clear that the Winnipeg strike was a move to gain better wages and a wider acceptance of collective bar-

The effects of the Winnipeg Strike are not summarized in the numbers of those injured and arrested. Nor did it lead to immediate concessions to organized labour. To radicals the strike was a failure; to the more moderate leaders in the labour movement it was a clear indication that other means were needed to voice the grievances of workingmen.

gaining, rather than a seditious plot to bring about a Communist form of government. But there is little doubt that it struck terror into the hearts of many, or that it left wounds in Winnipeg which would continue to fester for a long, long time.

"C'est fini"

As that decade drew to a close, three of the principal actors who had held centre stage during those tumultuous ten years made their exits.

Laurier, the essentially gentle man who had known little but tumult in his political life, survived two strokes but died of a third. On the seventeenth of February, 1919, clasping his wife's hand as she sat at his bedside, he whispered *"C'est fini"* and closed his eyes for the last time.

Henri Bourassa, with thirty-three more years of life ahead of him, retired to a long twilight of quiet observation, somehow lost now that he no longer had Sir Wilfrid to provide counterpoint to his opinions. "He knows that, although I fought him because of differences of principle, I loved him all my life," the publisher of *Le Devoir* noted sadly, on learning of Laurier's death.

Borden, who had unstintingly exhausted his limited physical strength, first in directing the war effort, and then in fighting for, and winning Canada's right to a full partnership in the peace settlements, announced his desire to retire from public life. Having stayed on reluctantly for some months, he was finally permitted to resign in the summer of 1920.

Waiting in the wings were the new leaders – William Lyon Mackenzie King, Arthur Meighen and J.S. Woodsworth.

And the back-drop would be that of the confident, prosperous, often frantic, sometimes silly, bathtub gin, flapper world of the 1920s.

The funeral cortège of a great statesman files past Ottawa's Parliament Hill. On Feb. 17, 1919, Wilfrid Laurier ended his career with the words, "C'est fini."

Acknowledgements

To whatever extent *The Years of Agony* contributes significantly to an understanding of the Canadian heritage, it owes a great deal to many people who have made it possible.

Among them are the newspaper editors and reporters of the period; those who have written local and regional histories (most of them superbly done), without which the Canadian story could never be compiled; and dozens of quite extraordinary men and women who gave generously of their personal recollections of this dramatic, demanding and formative decade. I hope I have been worthy of their trust. And, to all of them, my heartfelt thanks.

I am also grateful to Hurtig Publishers for permission to quote the extract on page 108 herein from their publication *Edmonton*, by J.G. MacGregor, 1967.

John Craig

The Author

The son of a newspaper editor, John Craig was born in Peterborough, Ontario. He received a B.A. from the University of Manitoba, and an M.A. in Canadian History and International Relations from the University of Toronto in 1951. In 1969, he left a seventeen-year career in marketing and opinion research to become a full-time writer. He has written more than twenty books, including novels, non-fiction and books for children. One of his novels was made into the CBS Movie of the Week, *Your Money or Your Wife*, and a second, *In Council Rooms Apart*, is also being made into a film. Other titles include *The Noronic Is Burning!*, *Some of My Best Friends Are Fishermen*, and *The Crazy Twenties*, a volume in Canada's Illustrated Heritage.

Index

125

Picture Credits

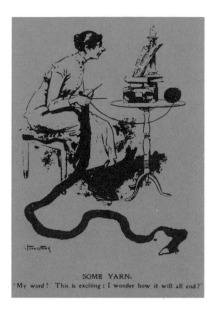

SOME YARN.
"My word! This is exciting; I wonder how it will all end?"

We would like to acknowledge the help and co-operation of the directors and staff of the various public institutions and the private firms and individuals who made available paintings, posters, mementoes, collections and albums as well as photographs and gave us permission to reproduce them. Every effort has been made to identify and credit appropriately the sources of all illustrations used in this book. Any further information will be appreciated and acknowledged in subsequent editions.

The illustrations are listed in the order of their appearance on the page, left to right, top to bottom. Principal sources are credited under these abbreviations:

ANQ   Archives Nationales du Québec
CWM   Canadian War Museum, National Museum of Man, National Museum of Canada
GA   Glenbow-Alberta Institute
JC   James Collection of Early Canadiana, City of Toronto Archives
MTCL   Metropolitan Toronto Central Library
NMST   National Museum of Space & Technology, Aviation and Space Division, Ottawa
PAC   Public Archives of Canada
PAM   Provincial Archives of Manitoba
RCMI   Royal Canadian Military Institute

/1 MTCL, Fine Arts Dept., Pat Rogul /2 RCMI /4 Confederation Life /6 PAC C 2533 /7 *Young Canada* /8 *6th Battery C.F.A. Overseas* /9 Private collection /10 Toronto Transit Commission /11 Rous & Mann Archives /12 GA; Vancouver City Archives /13 JC; Canadian Motorist Publishing Co., Ltd. /14 Eaton's Archives /15 Private collection /16 Eaton's Archives; ANQ /17 GA; Private collection; JC; JC /18 United Church Archives /19 Foote Collection, Manitoba Archives /20 *Canada Monthly*; Archives of British Columbia /21 Canadian Automotive Museum /22 Eaton's Archives; Larry Sherk /23 T. Kiil, Private collection /24 Edward Moogk, National Library, Ottawa /25 Titus Gallery, Victoria /26 Private collection /27 JC /28 GA; PAC C 14082 /29 University of Toronto Library /30 Private collection; Eaton's Archives /31 Canadian Motorist Publishing Co., Ltd.; *Calgary Eye Opener* /32 Alexandra Studio Archives /33 Provincial Archives of Alberta, E. Brown Collection /34 Provincial Archives, Victoria, B.C.; Alexandra Studio Archives /35 Alexandra Studio Archives; Private collection; PAC C 20932 /36

Alexandra Studio Archives /37 Mrs. Chas. L. Shields; *Saturday Night Scrapbook* /38 PAC T 432H /39 Norm Johnson Collection /40 Private collection /41 PAC C 4745 /42 ANQ /43 *Maclean's*; *Maclean's*; *Saturday Night Scrapbook*; *Saturday Night Scrapbook* /44 *Maclean's* /45 *Sunshine Sketches of a Little Town*; *Sunshine Sketches of a Little Town*; PAC C 7869 /46-47 All from McMichael Conservation Collection, Kleinburg, Ontario /48 John Ross Robertson Collection, MTCL /49 Mrs. Chas. L. Shields /50 *The Guide – A Manual for the Canadian Militia* /51 JC; JC /52 *The Guide*; Provincial Archives of Alberta, E. Brown collection. /53 Nova Scotia Museum, Marine Collection; Peterborough Centennial Museum /54 *Canada Monthly* /55 ANQ /56 PAC PA 2162 /57 Titus Gallery, Victoria /58 RCMI /59 RCMI /60 RCMI; Public Archives of Nova Scotia /61 RCMI; RCMI; PAC PA 3811 /62 Peterborough Centennial Musuem /63 *Maclean's* /64 *Canada Monthly* /65 CWM /66 CWM; CWM /67 CWM /68 CWM /69 *Saturday Night Scrapbook* /70 All from Thomas A. Gibson /71 PAC C 5470; Nova Scotia Museum, Halifax /72 *Montreal Star*; Dalhousie University Archives, Killam Memorial Library, Dalhousie University, Halifax, N.S. /73 Titus Gallery, Victoria; Private collection /74 PAC C 18734; Nora Bain /75 Manitoba Archives; JC; *Saturday Night Scrapbook* /76 GA /77 Provincial Archives of B.C. /78-79 MTCL /80 RCMI /81 Private collection /82 RCMI /83 RCMI /84 RCMI; Alan R. Capon Collection; RCMI; RCMI /85 RCMI; PAC PA 2316; RCMI; RCMI /86 PAC C 9040; ANQ; *Saturday Night Scrapbook*; PAC C 9021 /87 Dalhousie University Archives, Killam Memorial Library, Dalhousie University, Halifax, N.S. /88 *Saturday Night Scrapbook*; CWM; CWM /89 *Everywoman's World*; *Maclean's*; *Canada Monthly* /90 Rous & Mann Press /91 National Gallery and *Weekend Magazine* /92 RCMI /93 *Saturday Night Scrapbook* /94 *Canada Monthly*; Department of National Defence /95 PAC PA 2792; *The Varsity Magazine Supplement*, University of Toronto /96 PAC PA 1675 /97 Both from Victoria City Archives /98 RCMI; Mrs. Chas. L. Shields; NMST /99 PAC PA 2796 /100 RCMI /101 PAC PA 2789 /103 Titus Gallery, Victoria /104 *The Maple Leaf* /105 RCMI /106 GA; Fenelon Falls Museum /107 Ontario Emergency Volunteer Health Auxiliary /108 *Saturday Night Scrapbook* /109 Public Archives of Ontario /110 McMichael Conservation Collection, Kleinburg, Ontario; Art Gallery of Ontario; Max Merkur Collection /111 National Gallery of Canada /112 All from Nabisco Foods /113 Private collection /114 Provincial Archives of Alberta #71.300 /115 NMST #3525; PAC C 14677 /116 NMST #6706 /117 *Saturday Night Scrapbook* /118 T. Eaton Co., Ltd. Archives /119 Private collection /120 PAM; PAM; *Western Labor News* /121 PAM; PAM, Foote Collection; PAM /122 PAM /123 PAC PA 24973 /128 *Canada and Khaki*

1915

Saskatchewan first province to pass Prohibition.

First domestic war loan issued.

Canadian First Division holds Ypres when Germans first use chlorine gas as a weapon of war.

Machine guns successfully mounted on airplanes for air warfare.

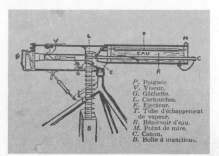

Percy Page organizes the Edmonton Grads, ladies basketball team.

Ontario implements Workmen's Compensation Act.

John McCrae publishes "In Flanders Fields" in *Punch*.

1916

First women to vote in Canada mark ballot in Alberta's municipal and civic elections.

Edmonton's Emily Murphy becomes first female police magistrate in the British Empire.

Sir Julian Byng takes command of Canadian Corps in Europe.

Duke of Devonshire appointed governor general.

During Battle of the Somme, British first use tanks.

Alberta Provincial Police formed.

Institute of Technology and Art established in Calgary.

Parliament Buildings in Ottawa destroyed by fire.

Montreal Canadiens win their first Stanley Cup.

Sam Hughes resigns as minister of militia and defence.

Duncan Campbell Scott publishes *Lundy's Lane and Other Poems*.

Railway Inquiry Commission recommends government takeover of Canadian Northern, Grand Trunk and Grand Trunk Pacific Railways.

1917

Imperial War Cabinet gives Canada voice in war management.

Compulsory Military Service Act becomes law.

Federal income tax introduced as a temporary wartime measure.

Prime Minister Borden heads Union Government after his Military Service Act splits Laurier's Liberals.

Gen. Arthur Currie takes command of Canadian Corps.